The Economics of Migration of Highly Skilled Workers from Türkiye

Hasan Gürak
Editor

The Economics of Migration of Highly Skilled Workers from Türkiye

The New Age of Colonialism

palgrave
macmillan

Editor
Hasan Gürak
Independent Researcher
Istanbul, Türkiye

ISBN 978-3-032-10605-6 ISBN 978-3-032-10606-3 (eBook)
https://doi.org/10.1007/978-3-032-10606-3

This Palgrave Macmillan imprint is published by the registered company Springer Nature Switzerland AG.
The registered company address is: Gewerbestrasse 11, 6330 Cham, Switzerland

Those who have knowledge
owe it to those who do not have it.
An old Turkish proverb

Preface

The migration of highly skilled professionals to developed countries (DCs) imposes a significant cost on developing countries (LDCs). This trend deprives LDCs of their most valuable asset: their skilled laborers.

If this pattern continues, how can LDC-economies realistically hope to catch up with developed nations? From a global justice perspective, is it fair, or rational, to overlook the challenges posed by the migration of highly skilled laborers, which clearly disadvantages LDCs?

To prevent further deepening global inequalities, collective action is needed to mitigate the adverse effects of the brain drain on developing countries. This book addresses this urgent issue by integrating perspectives with a particular focus on the challenges faced by Türkiye.

While there is extensive literature on "brain drain" and the "migration of labor," this book adopts a distinctive approach. It analyzes the issue from the perspective of developing countries, offering fresh insights into its impacts and implications.

A fundamental question must be asked in the pursuit of a more equitable global order: Who needs highly skilled laborers more, developed or developing countries?

The following questions are central to the book's inquiry:

- What are the primary factors driving the emigration of highly skilled individuals?
- How do variables such as education level, gender, and age correlate with migration patterns?
- What is the economic magnitude of this loss for LDCs?

- How many doctors and nurses have emigrated over the past five to ten years? What is the financial cost of their education in LDCs? What is the *opportunity cost* of their education for the countries that receive them?
- How many engineers, technicians, IT professionals, and AI experts have emigrated in the same period? What are the financial and opportunity costs of their training for both source and destination countries?
- What measures can or should LDCs adopt to prevent the permanent loss of highly qualified professionals?
- Conversely, what responsibilities do developed countries (DCs) have in regulating the inflow of such people?
- What can DCs do to support the development of skilled individuals in LDCs?
- Is reversing the brain drain a realistic objective for developing countries? If so, how might it be achieved?

To guide the analysis, I have formulated five core research questions:

- **Q1:** What is the overall scale of loss experienced by developing countries due to skilled migration? Who are the migrants in terms of education, age, gender, and destination? What are the driving forces behind this trend, and what is the estimated economic cost?
- **Q2:** How many doctors and nurses have emigrated in the past decade? What is the financial cost of their education for LDCs, and what is the opportunity cost for the receiving countries?
- **Q3:** How many IT professionals and AI experts have emigrated over the last ten years? What are the associated financial and opportunity costs?
- **Q4:** How many engineers and technicians have left in the same period? What are the implications for their countries of origin and for the countries benefiting from their labor?
- **Q5:** What policy measures can LDCs take to retain highly skilled professionals? What measures should DCs consider helping mitigate the negative consequences of talent extraction?

In 2024, my long-standing interest in these questions led me to initiate a book project as editor, drawing on contributions from countries such as Türkiye, India, Southern Africa, and Northern Africa. Despite the efforts of several scholars, many were unable to complete and submit their chapters on time.

Consequently, in 2025, I adopted a new strategy: instead of compiling articles into a single volume, I decided to produce a series of country-specific books. The first volume, now in your hands, focuses on Türkiye. Subsequent volumes will follow, each dedicated to another country.

What Distinguishes This Volume from Other Migration Studies?

1. This study is rooted in the theoretical framework presented in H. Gürak's 2024 book, *The Economic Value of Creative Mental Labor*. Key ideas include:
   - (a) Long-term economic growth is primarily driven by technological advancement.
   - (b) Creative Mental Labor (CML) is the sole source of technological progress.
   - (c) Skilled Mental Labor (SML) is essential for the effective utilization of any technology.
   - (d) Brain drain deprives developing countries of their most vital resource—skilled labor.
2. In a 2024 article published in *Pluto Journal*, Gürak characterizes the migration of highly skilled individuals as *The New Age of Colonialism*.
3. There remains a significant gap in the migration literature that critically examines brain drain from the standpoint of developing countries.
4. This research project involves a series of case studies, each based on a shared set of guiding questions to enable comparative cross-country analysis.
5. Predetermined questions are essential for drawing international comparisons, diagnosing common challenges, and formulating coherent policy responses.

It is important to clarify that this analysis does not encompass temporary student or academic exchanges. Furthermore, migration driven by marriage, political persecution, or cultural factors lies outside the scope of this study.

Plan of the Book

The content of the book can be divided into two parts. The first part, Chap. 1, contains Hasan Gürak's "general" analysis, views, criticism, and suggestions of all countries regarding migration of highly skilled workers. In the second part, Chaps. 2–6 contain concrete analyses and proposals regarding migration from Türkiye.

Chapter 1, titled "The New-Age Imperialism: Perspectives from Developing Countries on the Exploitation of Highly Educated Workers," examines the consequences of the migration of highly educated individuals from LDCs to DCs such as those in Europe, North America, Japan, Australia, and New Zealand. While DCs understand the economic value of skilled labor and actively attract it, the pressing question remains: who advocates for the needs and rights of developing countries' citizens?

Gürak refers to this process as *New-Age Imperialism* (NAI), with the benefiting countries described as *Contemporary Imperialists* (CI).

Chapter 2 analyzes the growing brain drain from Türkiye, exploring both global and domestic factors. Drawing on migration theories such as the push-pull model, network theory, the center of attraction concept, and the macro-meso-micro framework, the chapter identifies push factors including political instability, declining meritocracy, poor working conditions, and economic downturns. Pull factors include better job prospects, living standards, and professional recognition abroad. While Türkiye has introduced limited return incentives, they remain inadequate. The authors argue for more effective, merit-based policies and structural reforms.

Chapter 3 focuses on the migration of healthcare professionals from Türkiye. It assesses the broader global implications of healthcare-related brain drain and highlights the unequal dynamics of global mobility. Since the 2000s, the trend has accelerated, especially in the healthcare sector. Germany, the United States, and the United Kingdom are major destinations for Turkish professionals. The outflow exacerbates shortages in underserved regions and results in major financial losses due to the high cost of medical education.

Chapter 4 addresses the emigration of engineers and technicians. Despite substantial public investment in education and training, Türkiye reaps little return when these professionals emigrate. The loss hampers innovation, reduces productivity, and threatens long-term economic growth by depleting critical human capital. High-tech sectors suffer from skill shortages, weakening competitiveness and discouraging foreign investment. The chapter also explores the potential role of the Turkish diaspora in mitigating these effects. Long-term solutions include political and economic stability, educational reform, and proactive career development policies.

Chapter 5 takes a deeper look at the emigration of IT professionals and AI experts, emphasizing both the financial cost of their education and the opportunity costs for both source and destination countries. It presents a detailed account of migration trends and concludes with policy recommendations to reduce the outflow and enhance retention of skilled professionals in Türkiye.

Chapter 6 synthesizes the findings of the previous chapters and offers forward-looking policy recommendations from a developing-country perspective. Its core message is clear:

Developing countries need highly skilled professionals more than developed countries.

Istanbul, Türkiye
2025

Hasan Gürak

Note: The views expressed in this book are those of the individual authors and do not necessarily reflect the views of the editor or affiliated institutions.

Contents

Notes on Contributors

Yiğit Cem Eskicioğlu is currently pursuing his PhD in International Relations, focusing on the Turkish diaspora. He works as a research assistant at the Center for Diaspora Studies at Sakarya University. His research interests include diaspora studies, collective memory, foreign policy, and imperialism.

Haşmet Gökırmak is an associate professor at Istanbul Sabahattin Zaim University. He received his MA degree in international economics from Georgetown University (Washington, D.C.) in 1991 and his PhD degree in economics from American University (Washington, D.C.) in 1995. Gökirmak has worked as a professional manager for transportation and media companies for more than twenty-five years. His current areas of research include logistics and transportation, international trade, international finance, and energy economics.

Hasan Gürak is an economist known for his works on alternative theories of growth and value-price, as well as critiques of established economic thinking. His writings aim to develop more realistic and culturally grounded approaches to economics.

Zehra Hopyar holds a PhD in Sociology (2023) from Sakarya University. During her postgraduate studies, she spent a year at the London School of Economics and Political Science (LSE), where she was a research fellow at the Division of Modern Turkish Studies. She is currently a faculty member in the Department of Sociology at Bursa Uludağ University. Her research focuses on diaspora studies, return migration, skilled migration, transnational studies, and everyday life experiences.

Fuat Sekmen is Professor of Economics at Sakarya University. He earned his master's degree in Economics from American University (Washington, D.C.) and completed his PhD in Economics at George Mason University (Fairfax, Virginia) in 2004. He joined the Department of Economics at Sakarya University in the same year. His primary research interests lie in the fields of macroeconomics, monetary economics, international finance, applied econometrics, and development economics.

Soner Tauscher received his PhD from Sakarya University with a dissertation on human rights and biopolitics, after completing his undergraduate and graduate studies at Ludwig-Maximilian University of Munich. He is currently a faculty member in the Department of International Relations at Sakarya University and Director of the Center for Diaspora Studies. His research focuses on international migration, the far right, postcolonial theory, diaspora, and Islamophobia.

Fikret Topal is a political scientist whose research primarily focuses on political parties, party systems, political institutions, and Turkish political life. He has published on various aspects of political parties and comparative politics, contributing to the broader understanding of political development in Türkiye.

List of Figures

List of Graphs

List of Tables

CHAPTER 1

The New-Age Imperialism: Perspectives from Developing Countries on the Exploitation of Highly Educated Workers

Hasan Gürak

Introduction

Let's start by defining what I mean by the "**New Age of Imperialism**[1]" (**NAI**). I use the term Imperialism to refer to the **exploitation of resources in the less developed or developing countries (LDCs)**. Traditionally, more advanced countries (**DCs**) not only exploited resources such as raw

[1] Imperialism and colonialism are often conflated and used interchangeably. In this chapter, imperialism is defined as a policy or practice by which a nation, typically a developed country (DC) and DC-firms, expands its power through control or influence over the resources and economic policies of other nations, primarily developing countries (LDCs). In contemporary global relations, an unequal economic structure, rooted in the technological, organizational, and intellectual labor advantages of DCs, often exacerbates inequality and reinforces dominance. This dynamic is frequently facilitated by **global value chains (GVCs),** which I refer to as **instruments of new-age imperialism.**

H. Gürak (✉)
Independent Researcher, Istanbul, Türkiye

H. Gürak (ed.), *The Economics of Migration of Highly Skilled Workers from Türkiye*,
https://doi.org/10.1007/978-3-032-10606-3_1

materials and laborers but also controlled domestic markets and output in developing countries (**LDCs**). In our age, **the new age of Imperialism** (exploitation) in economic terms continues in various forms such as:

1. Exploitation of the LDCs' most valuable assets, i.e., **migration of skilled labor**.
2. Exploitation through **imperfections in technology markets**.

I previously examined the imperfections within technology markets in detail (see Gürak, 2012, chapter 9). Here, I turn my attention to another critical issue: the migration of skilled labor from LDCs, with a particular focus on the migration of highly educated professionals, especially in the fields of technology and healthcare.

Having defined the New Age of Imperialism, I will now begin my analysis by categorizing countries into two broad groups, as detailed below:

1. Countries that invent/innovate and implement new technologies, e.g., **DCs**, and
2. Countries that use, in general, existing technologies, e.g., **LDCs**.

Consequently, **DCs** are generally those countries that create new products and/or new process methods through technological inventions/innovations. **DCs**, owing to their advanced stage of development, are also the nations with the human resources capable of effectively harnessing existing and emerging technologies.

LDCs, on the other hand, can mainly be defined as countries that mainly attempt to use existing technologies effectively, which means that the biggest requirement for **LDCs** is not **Creative Mental Labor (CML)** that creates new technologies but **Skilled Mental Labor (SML)** that uses existing technologies effectively (see Gürak, 2024b, for details about **CML** and **SML**).

Aim and Scope of the Study

In this chapter, the focus of analysis will be on the migration of highly educated professionals. Specifically, two key groups of individuals holding

Accordingly, this chapter uses the term **new-age imperialism** to describe these exploitative relationships and the global economic-political system that disproportionately benefits DCs and their corporations.

tertiary-level diplomas will be examined: medical doctors and information technology (**IT**) experts. The analysis aims to explore the underlying motives driving their migration, the magnitude of this phenomenon, and the economic implications of their departure for the home country.

The geographical scope of this study is confined to Türkiye, serving as a case study to illuminate the challenges and potential solutions associated with the migration of highly skilled individuals. This focus is particularly relevant as all developing countries face similar issues—namely, the systematic depletion of their most valuable resources: highly educated brains.

It is important to clarify that this study does not encompass temporary scientific exchanges or student mobility, as these fall outside its scope.

Critical Questions

- How big is the loss of Türkiye expressed in the **numbers of highly skilled migrants**?
- What measures can or should Türkiye take to **prevent the migration of highly qualified brains**?
- What measures can or should **DCs** take to **prevent the emigration of highly qualified brains into their countries**?
- Would it be possible to **"reverse the brain drain"**[2]? How?

In this short chapter, I do not attempt to provide definitive answers to the critical questions outlined above. Instead, the primary aim of this work is to lay the groundwork for future research on the migration of highly skilled professionals.

On the Importance of Highly Skilled Persons in Economic Growth

It is a widely acknowledged fact that human intellect, referred to in this work as "skilled mental labor", represents both the inexhaustible source and the ultimate steward of knowledge within every nation.[3]

[2] See Appendix 1.

[3] **The total labor force**, denoted by the letter **L**, consists of two categories:

1. **Creative Mental Labor (CML) inventing/innovating technologies,** i.e., ($\mathbf{L}^{CM}$), and

Careful observations and analysis reveal that nations with higher levels of general and higher education consistently achieve superior living standards. While the development of "general knowledge" holds undeniable importance, the true determinant of global living standards lies in the advancement of **"new productive knowledge"**—specifically, **knowledge related to new production methods and/or the creation of new products, i.e., new technologies**. From the perspective of economic growth and development, access to "productive knowledge" and a properly qualified labor force emerges as an indispensable prerequisite, a sine qua none for sustained progress.[4]

2. **Skilled Mental Labor (SML) implementing technology,** i.e., **(L^{SM})** (Gürak, 2024a).

SML can be further divided into three sub-categories:

1. **The highly skilled labor (SML^{hs})** consists of people educated in high-tech implementation fields, such as engineers, technicians, AI, and IT experts, including doctors and nurses.
2. **The skilled labor (SML^{s})** consists of those who have obtained vocational school-level or equivalent education.
3. **The ordinary skilled labor (SML^{o})** comprises the rest of the total labor force, equipped with "general" knowledge acquired through formal and informal education. No labor is zero-skilled.

To put it differently, **L** comprises **CML, SML^{hs}, SML^{s},** and **SML^{o}.**

Or **L= (CML + SML)**

$$L = (L^{CM} + L^{SM})$$

Although **technology inventing CML** is essential to long-run economic growth and the reason the rate of profit does not fall to zero, as predicted by Marx, it will be outside the scope of our analysis. The brain drain of **highly skilled labor (L^{hs}) with tertiary-level qualification from LDCs** is the focus of our analysis.

The concept of "human capital" denoted by **"H"** refers to the talent, skills, and experience of the laborer. Yet, in economic analysis, it is used as if it is "a distinct part" of the factor of production, the "capital". This perspective is both flawed and misleading. If it pertains to the labor of the worker, why then label it as "capital" unless there is an underlying ideological motivation to do so? Such terminology appears to obscure the distinction between labor and capital, which potentially serves an ideological agenda rather than reflecting an accurate economic or social reality (see Gürak, 2024a, *The Economic Value of Creative Mental Labor*, Palgrave Macmillan and also Gürak, 2012 and 2015).

[4] To focus solely on migration, I intentionally set aside considerations of "institutional and infrastructural deficiencies" as well as "technology market imperfections". For a detailed analysis of "technology market imperfections", see H. Gürak, 2003, (PDF), Hidden Costs of Technology Transfer (researchgate.net)

What is the standard of general and specific vocational education in **DCs** and **LDCs**? As is widely recognized, there exists a significant disparity in development levels between nations, which is mirrored in the vast differences in living standards. The critical question, therefore, is whether this gap—both in terms of development and access to a properly educated labor force—is narrowing or widening over time.

The role of highly skilled labor inputs in the development process aimed at achieving the standards of **DCs** is both significant and undeniable. While decision-makers in **LDCs** implement various measures and strategies to mitigate and eventually eliminate these disparities, they face significant challenges. The institutional infrastructure, the quality and quantity of educational personnel, and the availability of educational materials in developing countries, including Türkiye, remain insufficient and inadequate to meet these ambitious goals.

Insufficiencies and/or deficiencies within the educational infrastructure are not the sole issue. In particular, the most highly educated individuals, notably those with promising futures, often opt to leave their less developed countries in pursuit of improved living standards elsewhere. Regrettably, these indispensable resources—arguably the sine qua non of development—are continually and systematically siphoned off by **DCs**, exacerbating inequalities and hindering the progress of **LDCs**.

The approach of **DCs** to the migration of highly skilled individuals is of paramount importance. In principle, they have often been inclined to prevent the mobility of low-qualified or unqualified individuals from **LDCs**. However, **DCs** that strongly object to the mobility of low qualified individuals, radically change their standpoint when the issue is the migration of highly qualified **LDCs**. In other words, whenever **DCs** perceive a distinct advantage that can enhance their own interests, they swiftly alter their principles (restrictions) and become exceptionally accommodating, establishing suitable avenues for the migration of highly qualified individuals.[5] Unfortunately, the negative implications of migration for **LDCs**

[5] "*Drawing on the new DEMIG POLICY database that comprises over 6,500 migration policy changes in 45 countries ... The findings challenge the common assumption that migration policies have become increasingly restrictive over the past decades and instead demonstrate that since 1945 migration policies have been consistently dominated by less restrictive changes. ... the essence of post-WWII migration policies has been an increasing sophistication through the development of specific policy instruments targeting particular immigrant groups. While policies towards migrant categories such as irregular migrants and, more recently, family members have often become more restrictive, a larger number of—generally less visible—policies targeting high*

often appear to be disregarded or deemed inconsequential in the broader dynamics of this process.

Access to highly skilled brains is an essential and irreplaceable input for supplying modern products and generating wealth in all nations. Unfortunately, **LDCs** are continuously losing their most valuable assets required for economic growth and development, i.e., the "highly educated" individuals to **DCs**. This process can be called a new wave of "**New-Age Imperialism**" or "**Neo Imperialism**".

A century ago, under the system of Imperialism, **DCs** exerted control over both the sources of raw materials and labor inputs as well as the consumer markets in colonial territories, prioritizing their own interests and, when necessary, employing force to maintain this dominance. Today, however, such overt coercion is no longer required to extract the most valuable resources—namely, the "highly educated" individuals—from **LDCs**. Migration has become the modern mechanism through which these highly skilled individuals are transferred at minimal cost possible. The financial and logistical burden of their education and training remains squarely on the shoulders of **LDCs**, yet it is the **DCs** that reap the benefits. Furthermore, **DCs** do not indiscriminately absorb educated individuals but selectively accept only the "**best and brightest**", tailored to their specific needs, further increasing the developmental challenges faced by **LDCs**.

Who can reasonably contend that DCs have a greater necessity for highly skilled labor than LDCs?

On Global Migration

Migration, in general, from **LDCs** to **DCs** is an important and global issue that needs to be addressed urgently.

> *The UNDESA[6] estimates the stock of international migrants worldwide at 272 million, of which 245 million are of working age (aged 15 and over) in 2019.12 The stock of international migrant workers in the same year totals 169 million. The 2019 estimate is up by 5 million (3.0 per cent) from the 2017 estimate and by 19 million (12.7 per cent) as compared to the 2013 estimate.*

and low-skilled workers, students and migrants from specific origins have become less restrictive. Migration policies should therefore be understood as a tool of migrant selection rather than as an instrument affecting numbers" (de Haas et al., 2014, Abstract).

[6] UNDESA: United Nations Department of Economic and Social Affairs.

> *In 2019, international migrants constituted 4.3 per cent of the working age population (aged 15 and over) while migrant workers constituted 4.9 per cent of the labour force of destination countries. Despite the global rise in the number of migrant workers over time, their share among migrants of working age is decreasing. In 2013, migrant workers constituted 72.7 per cent of migrants of working age but 70.0 per cent in 2017 (ILO 2015 and 2018b). Their share in 2019 is estimated at 69.0 per cent. The decreasing share of migrant workers could be attributed to the continuous rise in the number of migrants of working age and a decline in their labour force participation.* (ILO, 2021, p. 20)

The trend of global migration is upward and seems to be accelerating due to economic poverty, inequality in global income distribution, wars/insurgencies around the world, and other causes.

> *The current United Nations estimate is that there are about 281 million international migrants in the world, which equates to 3.6 per cent of the global population. But increasing numbers of people are being displaced, within and out of their country of origin, because of conflict, violence, political or economic instability as well as climate change and other disasters. In 2022, there were 117 million displaced people in the world, and 71.2 million internally displaced people. The number of asylum-seekers has risen from 4.1 million in 2020 to 5.4 million in 2022, an increase of more than 30 per cent.* (IOM, 2024, Foreword) (see also Table 1.1)

Tens of millions of people have already migrated (see Table 1.2), and tens of millions of them are waiting in "crossroad" countries such as Türkiye, Morocco, Tunisia, and Mexico for an opportunity to cross the border.

The primary destinations for migrants are predominantly Western industrialized nations, alongside Russia and oil-rich states such as Saudi Arabia and the United Arab Emirates. Among these, the United States consistently occupies the leading position as the most sought-after destination (see Table 1.3).

Global Migration Trend of the Highly Skilled

In this section, I will concentrate on the migration statistics of individuals with tertiary-level education. To begin, let me examine the scale of migration for both low-educated and highly educated individuals from developing countries in the year 2000 (see Table 1.4). Approximately one-third of

Table 1.1 Key facts and figures from *World Migration Report* 2024

Estimated number of international migrants	281 million
Estimated proportion of world population who are migrants	3.6 percent
Estimated proportion of female international migrants	48.0 percent
Estimated proportion of international migrants who are children	10.1 percent
Region with the highest proportion of international migrants	Oceania
Country with the highest proportion of international migrants	The UAE
Number of migrant workers	169 million
Global international remittances (USD)	831 billion
Number of refugees	35.4 million
Number of internally displaced persons	71.4 million

Source: IOM World Migration Report (2024, p. 8, Table 1)

Notes: The dates of the data estimates in the table may be different to the report publishing date (refer to the reports for more detail on dates of estimates); refer to Chapter 3 of this report for regional breakdowns

Table 1.2 Top ten countries with the highest number of emigrants[a]

1	India	17.9 million
2	Mexico	11.1 million
3	Russia	10.8 million
4	China	10.5 million
5	Syria	8.5 million
6	Bangladesh	7.4 million
7	Pakistan	6.3 million
8	Ukraine	6.1 million
9	Philippines	6.1 million
10	Afghanistan	5.9 million

Source: World Population Review, UN (2020). https://worldpopulationreview.com/country-rankings/immigration-by-country, 2023.11.15

[a]An emigrant is someone who *left* their home country and moved somewhere else. World Population Review

the total migrants, amounting to 12,391 individuals, were highly educated professionals. This represents a substantial loss to **LDC**s countries, not only in terms of the financial investment in education but, more critically, in the loss of skilled labor essential for domestic production and economic growth.

For African countries, the situation is particularly dire concerning the migration of highly educated individuals. As illustrated in Table 1.5, Cape Verde tops the list with a staggering 82 percent of its highly educated population migrating, followed by Seychelles at 77 percent, Gambia at 68

Table 1.3 Top ten countries with the highest number of immigrants[a]

1	The United States	50.6 million
2	Germany	15.8 million
3	Saudi Arabia	13.5 million
4	Russia	11.6 million
5	The United Kingdom	9.4 million
6	The United Arab Emirates	8.7 million
7	France	8.5 million
8	Canada	8.0 million
9	Australia	7.7 million
10	Spain	6.8 million

Source: World Population Review, UN (2020). https://worldpopulationreview.com/country-rankings/immigration-by-country, 2023.11.16

[a]An immigrant is someone who *came to* the country where they now live from somewhere else. World Population Review

Table 1.4 Structure of migration (in thousands), 2000

	Total	*Low-skilled*	*High-skilled*
Developing countries	37,890	17,395	12,391

Source: Capuano, S. and Marfouk, A. (2013). "African Brain Drain and Its Impact on Source Countries", *Journal of Comparative Policy Analysis*, Vol. 15, No. 4, 298, Table 1

Note: Migrants are defined as people aged 25 or older. Low-skilled = persons with less than secondary diploma, high-skilled = persons with tertiary diploma

Table 1.5 Emigration (25 years and over) from some African to OECD countries, by country of origin; top ten ranked in decreasing order, year 2000

Country of origin	*High-skilled (in thousands)*	*Country of origin*	*High-skilled emigration rate (in percent)*
South Africa	173,411	Cape Verde	82
Morocco	155,994	Seychelles	77
Egypt	151,451	Gambia	68
Nigeria	148,780	Mauritius	56
Algeria	87,777	Sierra Leone	49
Kenya	80,287	Ghana	45
Ghana	67,105	Liberia	44
Ethiopia	52,538	Kenya	39
Tunisia	40,226	Uganda	36
Congo Dem. Rep.	38,017	Eritrea	35

Source: Capuano, S. and Marfouk, A. 2013. "African Brain Drain and Its Impact on Source Countries", *Journal of Comparative Policy Analysis*, Vol. 15, No. 4, 301, Table 2

Table 1.6 Top emigration countries of "tertiary-educated", 2010–2011, Emigration rate percent of total

Guyana	93.0
Haiti	75.1
Trinidad and Tobago	68.2
Barbados	66.1
Jamaica	48.1
Tonga	48.1
Mauritius	43.8
Zimbabwe	43.6
Congo	37.4
Malta	36.5

Source: OECD Database on Immigrants in OECD and non-OECD Countries DIOC/2010-11; in: "Migration and Remittances", Factbook 2016

percent, and Mauritius at 56 percent. This alarming trend gives the impression that African nations are inadvertently serving the interests of **DC**s, often to their own detriment. Meanwhile, DCs appear largely unperturbed—at least from an ethical standpoint—by the profound developmental consequences, this brain drain imposes on African nations.

There are countless examples from **LDC**s around the world similar to those in African countries. In 2010, Guyana topped the list with 93 percent followed by Haiti, 75 percent, and Trinidad and Tobago 68 percent (see Table 1.6).

Who cares, as long as the dynamics continue to favor the interests of developed and affluent nations?

Let me now shift our focus to examine the situation from the perspective of Türkiye.

Migration of the Highly Skilled from Türkiye

In this section, focus will be on two groups endowed with tertiary-level qualification: medical doctors (physicians) and information technology (**IT**) experts.

Medical Doctors (Physicians)

As is the case in almost all **LDC**s, there is a shortage of highly qualified healthcare personnel in Türkiye. This situation is partly due to inadequate training facilities and partly due to emigration abroad. When it comes to the migration of "highly skilled" individuals, doctors are undoubtedly at the top of the list. According to data from the Turkish Medical Association, as reported on the BBC Turkish[7] website, only 59 doctors applied to relocate abroad in 2012. However, this number has increased significantly, surpassing 1200 in the first 11 months of 2021. The number of doctors applying to the Turkish Medical Association for documentation to emigrate is rising daily, and this trend is concerning. In addition to doctors, a significant number of nurses, midwives, dentists, and other highly skilled healthcare professionals are also seeking opportunities to emigrate and are taking advantage of the first chance they get.

In this section, I will only consider medical doctors. First, let's start by comparing the data from Türkiye and Germany. The choice of Germany for comparison is not coincidental. Both Türkiye and Germany have comparable populations in 2024, with Türkiye about 85 million and Germany about 83 million. This demographic similarity makes Germany an ideal benchmark for comparative analysis among European Union countries.

According to the data presented in Table 1.7, based on figures from 2021, Germany had 376,900 doctors while Türkiye had only 183,600—nearly half of Germany's total (see Durmuş, 2023). This disparity indicates which country has a more pressing need for medical doctors. Türkiye faces a far greater and more urgent demand for doctors to meet its healthcare needs. However, Germany, like other **DC**s, adopts a highly self-serving approach, actively facilitating the immigration of Turkish doctors to strengthen its own healthcare system. Moreover, this process is selective, targeting the most skilled and highly qualified doctors, while leaving the less desirable ones to serve in Türkiye.

A highly admirable and ethical policy, in every sense of the word, isn't it?

More Than 6000 Syrian Doctors Work in Germany
Syrians make up the largest number of foreign doctors working in Germany over the past decade, with 6,120 physicians, according to a media report.

The report said that the number of doctors working in Germany without a German passport reached a significant total of 63,763 as of December 31, 2023.

Syria topped the list with 6,120 physicians, followed by Romania 4,668, Austria 2,993, Greece 2,943, Russia 2,941, and Türkiye 2,628.

North Press Agency

https://npasyria.com/en/111807/

Table 1.7 Number of doctors, 2021

Türkiye	183,600
Germany	376,900

Source: EURONEWS (2023), quoted from Durmuş (2023)

Table 1.8 Number of doctors per 100,000 inhabitants, 2021

Türkiye	218
Germany	453

Source: EURONEWS, 2023, quoted from Durmuş (2023)

The number of doctors per 100,000 inhabitants clearly shows how dire the situation is for Türkiye. While this number is 453 in Germany, it is 541 in Austria, 516 in Norway, 444 in Switzerland, and only 218 in Turkiye (see Table 1.8).

Similar situations to those in Türkiye also apply to other **LDC**s. Whether it is the United States, France or Sweden, all **DC**s are doing everything possible to transfer the wanted healthcare personnel from **LDC**s to their countries.

The critical question is: Is the health of people in DCs more valuable than the health of people in LDCs?

IT Experts

Regarding the migration of **IT** experts, I have heavily benefited from Metin and Ertan (2022).

> *A total number of 63,787 individuals from universities in Türkiye have received their bachelor's degrees from IT departments between 2004 and 2013. … through considering 7,287 bachelor's degree graduates abroad, the brain drain rate of Türkiye in the field of IT is calculated as 11.4 per cent in the year 2020.* (Metin & Ertan, 2022, p. 88)

Figure 1.1 shows the magnitude of brain drain of **IT** graduates for Türkiye for the years 2009–2020. There was an increasing trend from 7.4 percent in 2009 to 11.4 percent in 2020, which is clearly to the detriment of Türkiye's economic interests. Türkiye was losing while the recipient countries were reaping substantial gains.

Table 1.9 presents the number and brain drain rates of **IT** graduates categorized by academic departments. The highest brain drain rate, at

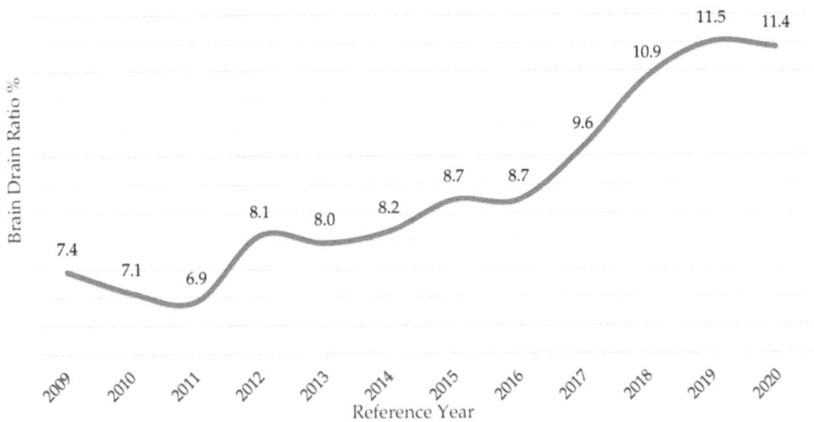

Fig. 1.1 Brain drain rates of IT graduates 2009–2020. (Source: F. Metin and H.T. Ertan, 2022, "The Brain Drain of IT Professionals: Register Evidence of Non-Return Graduates from Türkiye", p. 90, Figure 1)

29.8 percent—nearly one-third of graduates—was observed in the "*Computer Sciences and Engineering/Telecommunication*" field. This was followed by brain drain rates of 23.5 percent in "*Engineering/Computer Sciences/ Microeconomic Engineering*" and 21.5 percent in "*Control and Automation*". Undoubtedly, graduates from these departments represent a highly skilled and highly sought-after workforce, reflecting the critical loss of expertise for their home country.

Table 1.10 highlights the countries' preferences of **IT** experts. The United States leads by a substantial margin, attracting 26.6 percent of these professionals. Germany follows in second place with 14.9 percent, while the United Kingdom and the Netherlands closely trail with 11.4 percent and 11.2 percent, respectively. These figures reveal the dominant pull of Western industrialized nations in the global competition for top IT talent.

The Underlying Motive for Migration

What are the motives that drive people to migrate from LDCs? There are several reasons for migration, ranging from marriage, political persecution, cultural reasons to aspirations to live with a higher standard of living which can be described as "economic factors or motives". However, the

Table 1.9 Brain drain of IT graduates by departments, 2020

ISCED—F Code	*Departments*	*Number of graduates*	*Number of non-returned graduates*	*Brain drain rate (%)*
(0613/)	Computer Sciences and Eng./Telecommunications	1274	379	29.8
(0714)	Eng./ Computer Sciences /Microelectronic Engineering			
0714	Control and Automation Engineering	408	96	23.5
0714	Information Systems Engineering	483	104	21.5
0714	Mechatronics Engineering	1342	210	15.6
0613	Software Engineering	601	89	14.8
0714	Computer Engineering	24,158	3186	13.2
0714	Electronics Engineering	3973	432	10.9
0613	Computer Technologies and Information Systems	1010	108	10.7
0714	Electronics and Communication Engineering	3722	343	9.2
0613	Management Information Systems	1524	140	9.2
0714	Electrical and Electronic Engineering	24,332	2127	8.7
0714	Information Systems and Technologies	382	28	7.3
0714	Biomedical Engineering	578	42	7.3
	Total	63,787	7284	11.4

Source: F. Metin and H.T. Ertan, 2022, "The Brain Drain of IT Professionals: Register Evidence of Non-Return Graduates from Türkiye", p. 90, Table 5

dominant motive for mass migration appears to be **economic factors**, i.e., **the shortest way to enjoy the highest standards**. This motive of migrants is quite rational when compared to the mass migration of Europeans who fled to the United States to escape poverty and hunger in the 1800s. Why should LDC-citizens not try to do the same?

In addition, let us recall what the theories of Western scholars and economists impose in economics textbooks: "Capital and Labor(-er) should be mobile across countries, if global prosperity is to be maximized".

In our age, capital is able to move freely across the countries in "rose gardens without horns". What about the other factor, i.e., labor(-er)? Why is it not allowed to move freely, as the "valuable" Western theories

Table 1.10 Brain drain of IT graduates by country, 2020

Emigrated country	*Number of non-returned graduates*	*Brain drain ratio (%)*
The United States of America	1935	26.6
Germany	1082	14.9
The United Kingdom	833	11.4
The Netherlands	819	11.2
Canada	282	3.9
Sweden	226	3.1
Switzerland	184	2.5
The United Arab Emirates	182	2.5
Ireland	149	2.0
Belgium	146	2.0
Australia	129	1.8
France	103	1.4
Poland	93	1.3
Spain	89	1.2
Austria	80	1.1
Finland	79	1.1

Source: F. Metin and H.T. Ertan, 2022 "The Brain Drain of IT Professionals: Register Evidence of Non-Return Graduates from Türkiye", p. 91, Table 6

recommend? There is, of course, an exception for the highly educated people. The critical question is:

Who needs the highly qualified labor inputs (brains) more: DCs or LDCs?

What to Do?

How can **LDC** economies catch up with **DC**s if this trend of migration of highly skilled individuals persists? Is it fair and rational, from a global perspective, to disregard the problems arising from the migration of highly skilled laborers, which clearly harms developing countries?

Forcing the skilled laborers to stay at home does not seem to be a practical or applicable measure. Efforts to curb the migration of highly skilled individuals primarily motivated by economic prospects cannot be effectively implemented without **DC**-policymakers taking concrete measures to address and regulate the migration phenomenon.

Unfortunately, **DCs** do not seem to have any intentions or precautions to prevent the migration of highly skilled laborers from **LDCs**. As long as

DCs pursue an "open door" policy to meet their need for highly skilled laborers, there appears to be no way to stop migration.

Global action must be taken to mitigate the negative effects of the brain drain of highly skilled labor from **LDCs**, if the goal is to prevent further deterioration in global prosperity.

It is essential to clarify that this analysis excludes temporary student or scientist exchanges, as well as instances of migration motivated by factors such as marriage, political persecution, or cultural considerations. These circumstances fall outside the scope of this study and are not addressed in the current analysis.

A Suggestion for Short- and Medium-Term Strategy

DCs, such as the United States, Germany, France, and the United Kingdom, are well-positioned to address the phenomenon of "brain drain" by fostering the development of vocational training and higher education systems in **LDCs**. This can be achieved through strategic investments in "unconditional" financial support, organizational partnerships, and the transfer of pedagogical expertise to strengthen educational infrastructure in **LDCs**. By leveraging their extensive resources and institutional capabilities, **DCs** have the potential to catalyze sustainable global development, which will advance the well-being of **LDCs** and their populations.

When individuals in **LDCs** gain access to contemporary qualifications through initiatives supported by **DCs**, their professional trajectories may follow diverse paths. While some people in **LDCs** may seek opportunities abroad, others, for various reasons, may choose to remain within their home countries. Those who stay are often well-positioned to secure employment with wages that surpass the local average, thereby contributing to economic advancement and capacity building within their communities.

In a broader context, such efforts yield mutual benefits for both **DCs** and **LDCs**. The global labor market is enriched by a labor force equipped with modern skills, fostering economic growth, reducing inequality, and enhancing international interdependence. This approach therefore exemplifies how cooperative investment in human labor can drive a more inclusive and equitable global order.

Suggestions for Long-Term Strategies

Let's say the critiques/suggestions made in this chapter were found favorable by decision-makers of both **DCs** and **LDCs,** and that measures were initiated in favor of **LDCs**. In this case, would all barriers to growth and development in **LDCs** be removed, paving the way for income convergence? In other words, would all economic challenges in **LDCs** be resolved, ushering in "rosy days" for us?

Unfortunately, the answer to this critical question is NO.

With the prevention of the migration of highly skilled labor, the most significant change will occur within the potential of **LDCs**. There would be a more abundant highly skilled labor force ready for service, but who would harness this potential?

In most **LDCs**, there are no "domestic businesses and products with global competitiveness".[8] In such an economic environment, it would be the enterprises of **DCs** that seem to offer the most favorable working conditions for the highly skilled labor force, with Foreign Direct Investments (**FDIs**) being the ones to maximize per capita value-added productivity. However, due to **"global technology market imperfections"**, **FDIs** bring along various challenges alongside their benefits. The greatest issue, in fact, is the lack of a genuine technology transfer (see Gürak, 2012). Thus, **LDCs** will remain, in a sense, in a process of "economic colonization" by **DCs**, and their dependencies will continue, serving as a form of bondage in every aspect.

A different approach related to the ownership of technologies could radically alter the colonial-like situations of **LDCs**. If the ownership of technologies (patents) belongs to businesses that function as "independent profit units" and only engage in technological research, leasing their patented knowledge to all manufacturing companies worldwide without discrimination, both global competitions will increase, and all businesses worldwide will benefit. As a result, with increased global competition, consumers will benefit, global prosperity will rise, and the exploitation and income inequality stemming from technology ownership will decrease (see Gürak, 2024a, chapter 7).

[8] When conducting an assessment, we assume that the general level of education in **LDCs**, as well as their technological, financial, political, and cultural infrastructure, is structured in a way that does not impede the progress of their economy and development. Unfortunately, this is not a very realistic assumption. However, as it is not possible to address and examine all the significant factors in this part, we can only bring them to the forefront and emphasize their importance.

The Walls of Shame

The phrase **"Wall of Shame"** was first associated with the Berlin Wall, built to prevent East Germans from fleeing to the West.

Today, developed countries like the **United States and the European Union** are erecting new **"walls of shame"** to block so-called **"unwanted" migrants** from entering.

Now, the **EU** is planning yet another **"wall of shame,"** this time along the border between **Greece and Türkiye**.

But will these barriers truly stop migration from developing countries?

Would it not be more **rational and humane** to tackle the root causes of migration—by improving living conditions in these regions, instead of building physical walls?

Last but not least, the following steps, if properly taken, would improve the economic conditions in LDCs considerably:

- *Reversing the brain drain of migrants to "home" countries*
- *Brain drain: migration of highly skilled individuals from DCs to LDCs*
- *Brain drains of "senior citizens"*[9]

Concluding Remarks

In this chapter, I have emphasized that **the only factor of production** that provides **"long-term growth"** is **"creative mental labor"** (**CML**), the sole source of all technological inventions and/or innovations.

SML is a sine qua non input of production to implement existing and new technologies efficiently. In other words,

1. **CML** invents/innovates "new products" and "new methods of production" for given products.
2. **SML** provides the available and new technologies in production.

CML and **SML** are both "indispensable" inputs for the production of all kinds of goods and services.

[9] Qualified but retired or presently inactive in the labor market.

Although **CML**, from the perspective of mainly **DC**-based competitive firms, is important due to global competitive conditions, **SML** requirements are more intense and urgent in **LDCs**. In other words, for **LDC** economies to grow and reduce income inequality with **DC** incomes, an "efficient" implementation of "given" technologies is a prerequisite. Therefore, access to appropriate **SML** is vital in **LDCs**.

However, **LDCs** are increasingly losing their most valuable assets, **SMLs**, to **DCs** due to migration of highly skilled brains as a result of self-centered and unethical policies in **DCs**. If the migration trend of **SML** continues as it is today, **LDCs** will continue to suffer severe economic losses in terms of **SML**, while **DCs** will be the winners at the lowest possible cost. And the convergence of global incomes will remain a utopian wish.

I call the existing global migration process of highly skilled people the **"New Age of Imperialism"** (**NAC**), and the countries benefitting from this process are called **"Contemporary Colonialists"** (**CC**).

DCs are well aware of the economic value of highly skilled labor and therefore make every effort to transfer them to their countries to serve their people.

But what about the needs of developing country citizens?

Who will defend and care for their interests?

"Contemporary-Imperialism" must be prevented, and global measures must be taken to increase the number and qualifications of **SMLs** in **LDCs**.

A Troubling and Growing Global Social Problem Urgently Needs a Remedy

In the previous section, we analyzed the issue of the "new age of Imperialism" from the perspective of developing countries and examined which country has a greater need for "highly skilled" individuals. In this subsection, we will explore another issue that is just as crucial as growth and development: the rising xenophobia and even hostility toward migrants in developed countries. This problem is escalating rapidly and leading to social conflicts.

People from developing countries, much like Europeans did in the past, aspire to improve their living standards by migrating to countries such as the United States, Australia, and Canada. While their decision is **economically motivated** and rational, the world is no longer what it was 100–150 years ago. Many citizens of developed countries are reluctant to accept migrants due to economic concerns and do not want their country to serve as a **gateway to economic prosperity** for others. As a result, they are implementing various measures to restrict immigration from developing nations. In Germany, for example, parties like AfD have even proposed deporting immigrants who have already acquired German citizenship. Nevertheless, at the same time, they attempt to maintain an open-door policy for the immigration of "highly skilled" individuals, thereby applying a blatant double standard.

The **issue of unwanted migration** in our era does not appear to be slowing down; on the contrary, it is expected to intensify in the coming years and decades. This is because the existing global economic system continues to enrich developed countries while further impoverishing developing ones. In other words, global income distribution is worsening.

Solving this issue in the short term seems impossible. However, in the medium and long term, several measures can help improve global income distribution:

1. The economic loss caused by the migration of "highly skilled" individuals to developed countries should be mitigated.
2. "Reversing brain drain" to developing countries should be encouraged and supported.
3. Developed countries should contribute to the training of **skilled and highly skilled** workforces in developing nations.
4. Gürak (2015) proposed the establishment of a **new global order** for technology transfer based on GESITS in the production and use of technology. This call should be acknowledged and supported.

A **new global order** must be established with regard to the perspectives of developing countries to create a more equitable global economic system. However, this "new global order" should certainly not prioritize the highly praised "Global Value Chains" order promoted by developed countries.[10] To comprehend this and approach the issue with prudence for the sake of humanity and global prosperity, reading Gürak's 2003 article titled "Hidden Costs of Technology Transfer" will suffice.

[10] See Appendix 2.

Appendix 1

Quoted from the book entitled *Economic Growth and Development-2*, 2018, pp. 90–92 Hasan Gürak

1-a: Reversing the brain drain of emigrants to 'home' countries

There is a great potential for qualified human resources that the LDCs can utilize in the short term: the qualified emigrants living in DCs. If these people can be encouraged to return home to the emigrated country, they can make a significant contribution to the development of the LDC economy with the knowledge and experience acquired in the DCs. With proper assistance and guidance from an institutional infrastructure, this process of reversed brain drain can produce valuable results.

1-b: Brain-drain: Emigration from the DCs to the LDCs

The idea of the emigration of DC citizens to the LDCs might seem like an optimistic expectation at first. However, a 'temporary' emigration policy through appropriate institutions can easily be implemented. As a matter of fact, there are some highly educated volunteers already working in LDCs, organized by international and/or national institutions. Although 'temporary', they have the potential to make a considerable contribution to the development of the local economy and the country. The contributions of the voluntary but temporary emigrants can easily be extended to cover all areas of development.

1-c: Brain drains of 'senior citizens'[11]

As life expectancy increases, the number of retired people increases accordingly, implying that more and more highly educated and well-qualified people with experience are leaving the active labor force of the DCs. We will refer to them as 'senior citizens who have the potential to carry out active work. If the right policies are designed and implemented, these senior citizens with precious qualifications can still make a giant contribution to the development of LDCs as part-time or full-time, temporary or permanent personnel. Such policies would serve the interests of the LDCs and make these people feel that they can still be effective.

[11] Qualified but retired or presently inactive in the labor market.

Appendix 2

Global Value Chains (GVCs)

The Major Agents in the New Era of Imperialism
The Global Value Chains (GVC) approach emerged in the 1990s as a tool to analyze the transnational fragmentation of production. Pioneered by scholars like G. Gereffi, J. Humphrey, and T. Sturgeon, GVCs refer to global production networks of globally operating companies (GOFs) or alternatively, multinational corporations (MNCs), where different stages of production of goods and services are spread across multiple countries. These predominantly DC-based chains allow companies to specialize in specific tasks, such as design, production, marketing, and distribution, which are cost-saving and more efficient, in line with the global interests of the GOF, often harming developing countries' vital interests (see Gürak, 2003, Hidden Costs of Technology Transfer).

Key Aspects of GVCs

1. Different components of a product are manufactured in different countries based on comparative advantages. For example, a computer may have its design developed in Sweden, components from Taiwan, assembly in Mexico, and marketing in all over the world.
2. GOFs coordinate and control GVCs.
3. GVC frameworks often prioritize lead firms' strategies while marginalizing the role of states, laborers, and civil society in other countries.
4. Developing countries face barriers to moving up the value chain due to imperfections in global technology markets and intellectual property regimes (e.g., TRIPS).
5. GVCs do not infrequently lead to economic and political dependence.
6. Reinforces global income inequality.

GVCs are primary agents of exploitation, or rather Imperialism, in our time.

References

Arnot, M., Schneider, C., & Welply, O. (2013). Education, mobilities and migration: People, ideas and resources. Retrieved March 31, 2025, from https://www.tandfonline.com/doi/abs/10.1080/03057925.2013.822194,

Atte, F. (2020). The moral challenges of health care providers brain drain phenomenon. *Clinical Ethics, 16*(2), 67–73. https://doi.org/10.1177/1477750920946614

Bağlama, S. H., & Güngör, B. (2023). 'Imperialism and literature: An imperialism-oriented' reading of modern Turkish literature. *Journal of European Studies, 53*(3), 253–268. https://doi.org/10.1177/00472441231188782

Blecker, R. A., & Setterfield, M. 2019 *Heterodox macroeconomics: Models of demand, distribution and growth*. Edward Elgar Publishing. Retrieved November 2, 2024, from https://tr.z-lib.gs/book/5421152/be074a/heterodox-macroeconomics-models-of-demand-distribution-and-growth.html?dsource=recommend

Boutang, Y. M. (2011). *Cognitive capitalism*. Polity Press.

Brock, G., & Blake, M. (2015). *Debating brain drain: May governments restrict emigration?* Oxford University Press.

Brzozowski, J. (2008). Brain drain or brain gain? The new economics of brain drain—Reconsidered. http://ssrn.com/abstract=1288043. Retrieved March 30, 2025, from https://www.academia.edu/8153512/Brain_Drain_or_Brain_Gain_The_New_Economics_of_Brain_Drain_Reconsidered?auto=download&email_work_card=download-paper

Capuano, S., & Marfouk, A. (2013). African brain drain and its impact on source countries. *Journal of Comparative Policy Analysis, 15*(4), 297–314, Routledge. https://doi.org/10.1080/13876988.2013.813122

Carling, J. (1996). International labour migration: Consequences for countries of origin. Retrieved March 31, 2025, from https://www.academia.edu/2961115/International_labour_migration_Consequences_for_countries_of_origi n?auto=download&email_work_card=download-paper

CHP. (2021). *Beyin Göçü*. Çalıştay Raporu. Retrieved November 21, 2024, from https://chp.org.tr/yayin/beyn-gocu-raporu/Open

Christiaensen, L., Gonzalez, A., & Robalino, D. (2019). *Migration and jobs*. Policy Research Working Paper 8867. Retrieved April 1, 2025, from https://www.academia.edu/70670800/Migration_and_Jobs_Issues_for_the_21st_Century?auto=download&email_work_card=download-paper

de Haas, H., Natter, K., & Vezzoli, S. (2014). *Growing restrictiveness or changing selection?* IMI, Oxford University. Working Paper 96, July 2014. Retrieved March 8, 2024, from www.migrationinstitute.org/publications/wp-96-14

de Haas, H., et al. (2019). *International migration: Trends, determinants, and policy effects*. Scholarly Publications, Leiden University. Retrieved February 18, 2024, from https://scholarlypublications.universiteitleiden.nl/handle/1887/135782

Dilshad, S. A. (2019). How does mass immigration transform the destination societies? *Prizren Social Science Journal, 3*(3), 77–83. Retrieved November 23, 2024, from https://www.researchgate.net/publication/338525319_How_Does_Mass_Immigration_Transform_the_Destination_Societies
Durmaz, A. (2020). Diaspora as a source of human capital: The effects of the relationship between scientific Turkish diaspora and the homeland on reverse brain drain. *Migration and Development*, Routledge. https://doi.org/10.1080/21632324.2020.1816036
Durmuş, S. (2023). 'Doktor Beyin Göçü' Pusula—PUGAT. Retrieved November 23, 2024, from https://www.pugat.org/toplum/2023/11/22/doktor-beyin-gocu/
Ellerman, D. (2004). The dynamics of skilled labor migration: What can be done about the brain drain? Retrieved March 31, 2025, from https://www.academia.edu/54745822/The_Dynamics_of_Skilled_Labor_Migration_What_can_be_done_about_the_Brain_Drain?auto=download&email_work_card=download-paper
Esipova, N., Pugliese, A., & Ray, J. (2018). More than 750 million worldwide would migrate if they could. *GALLUP*. Retrieved February 18, 2024, from https://news.gallup.com/poll/245255/750-million-worldwide-migrate.aspx
Gereffi, G. (2019). *Global value chains and development: Redefining the contours of 21st century capitalism*. Cambridge University Press.
Giousmpasoglou, C., & Koniordos, S. (2025). Brain drain in higher education in Europe: Current trends and future perspectives. Chapter 7. Retrieved May 13, 2025, from https://core.ac.uk/download/pdf/82893107.pdf
Güllüpınar, F., & Kaçar-Tunç, G. (2023). Brain drain of health workers from Turkey to Germany and Its results: Possibilities of brain gain (pp. 109–114). Retrieved November 22, 2024, from https://play.google.com/books/reader?id=cKXoEAAAQBAJ&pg=GBS.PA108&hl=tr
Gürak, H. (2003, June). Hidden costs of technology transfer. *YK-Economic Review*; İstanbul.
Gürak, H. (2012). *Heterodox economics: Foundations of alternative*. Economics International Academic Publishers.
Gürak, H. (2015). *Economic growth and development*. International Academic Publishers.
Gürak, H. (2018). *Economic growth and development-2*. International Academic Publishers.
Gürak, H. (2024a). *The economic value of creative mental labor: Economic growth and the labor theory of value*. Palgrave Macmillan.
Gürak, H. (2024b). Plundering the skilled workforce: Depriving developing nations of their most valuable assets. *World Review of Political Economy, 15*(3). Retrieved November 10, 2024, from https://www.scienceopen.com/hosted-document?doi=10.13169/worlrevipoliecon.15.3.0003
Hardt, M., & Negri, A. (2000). *Empire*. Harvard University Press.

ILO. (2021). *Global estimates on international migrant workers International Labour Office*. ILO.

IMD. (2024). *World competitiveness booklet*. World Competitiveness Center. Retrieved November 20, 2024, from https://www.investchile.gob.cl/wp-content/uploads/2024/08/Booklet_WCY_2024.pdf

Iohest, O. (2007, June 13). Brain drain in developing countries. *The World Bank Economic Review*. Retrieved March 31, 2025, from https://www.academia.edu/14552286/Brain_Drain_in_Developing_Countries?auto=download&email_work_card=download-paper

IOM. (2008). Migration and development: Perspectives from the South. Retrieved March 26, 2025, from https://publications.iom.int/system/files/pdf/md_perspectives_from_the_south.pdf

IOM. (2024). World Migration Report 2024. Retrieved November 21, 2024, from https://worldmigrationreport.iom.int/msite/wmr-2024-interactive/

Mahroum, S. (2000). Highly skilled globetrotters: Mapping the international migration of human capital R&D Management 30, 1, 2000. Retrieved March 31, 2025, from https://www.academia.edu/88380311/Highly_skilled_globetrotters_mapping_the_international_migration_of_human_capital?auto=download&email_work_card=download-paper

MEB. (2024). PISA—OECD Ülke Özetleri 2022. Retrieved October 16, 2024, from https://odsgm.meb.gov.tr/meb_iys_dosyalar/2024_05/06144528_ulke_ozetleri_rapor.pdf

Metin, F., & Ertan, H.T. (2021[2022]). The brain drain of IT professionals: Register evidence of non-return graduates from Türkiye. *Boğaziçi Journal Review of Social, Economic and Administrative Studies, 36*(2), 80–99. https://doi.org/10.21773/boun.36.2.2. Retrieved November 22, 2024, from file:///C:/Users/PC/AppData/Local/Temp/MicrosoftEdge Downloads/9e9147b6-2712-4f4d-8a47-9a2f1528f4cc/TheBrainDrainofITProfessionals.pdf

OECD. (2000). Investing in Education Pays Rich Dividends, UNESCO/OECD Study Confirms - OECD, Retrieved November 26, 2023, from https://www.timeshighereducation.com/news/investingin-education-pays-rich-dividends-unesco/oecd-study-confirms/174806.article

OECD. (2023a). Education at a glance. e13bef63-en.pdf (oecd-ilibrary.org). Retrieved November 22, 2023, from

OECD. (2023b). International Migration Outlook 2023. International Migration Outlook 2023 | en | OECD. Retrieved November 22, 2023, from

PRB. (2004). *World population data sheet*. Population Reference Bureau. Retrieved October 15, 2024, from https://web.archive.org/web/20170329104249/; http://www.prb.org/pdf04/04worlddatasheet_eng.pdf

Sheikheldin, G., & Nyichomba, B. (2010). Engineering education, development and growth in Africa. *Scientific African, 6* (2019). Retrieved September 8, 2024, from https://www.academia.edu/83196106/Engineering_education_development_and_growth_in_Africa

Solimano, A. (2002). *Globalizing talent and human capital: implications for developing countries.* CEPAL, Economic Commission for Latin America and the Caribbean. Retrieved December 24, 2024, from https://www.academia.edu/125978042/Globalizing_Talent_and_Human_Capital_Implications_for_Developing_Countries

Strikwerda, C. (2008). Review: "Global Migration and the World Economy: Two Centuries of Policy and Performance". By T. J. Hatton & J. G. Williamson, 2005. Retrieved March 31, 2025, from https://www.academia.edu/115283104/Global_Migration_and_the_World_Economy_Two_Centuries_of_Policy_and_Performance_By_Timothy_J_Hatton_and_Jeffrey_G_Williamson_Cambridge_Mass_The_MIT_Press_2005_483_pp_50_00

TBV (Türkiye Bilişim Vakfı). (2023). Türkiye Akademik Diaspora Raporu: Beyin Göçünden Beyin Gücüne. Retrieved November 19, 2024, from https://www.tbv.org.tr/Content/userfiles/files/Diaspora_Raporu.pdf

The Migration Conference. (2023). *Book of Abstracts, 2023 Hamburg.* Transnational Press.

TTB (Turkish Doctors' Association). (2022–2024). Raporu. Retrieved November 18, 2024, from www.ttb.org.tr/C_Rapor/2022-2024/CR_2022-2024.pdf

Uğur, N. (2022). Great risk for education cost: Brain drain (Resident physicians case). https://doi.org/10.17942/sted.979463. Retrieved 21, 2024, from https://dergipark.org.tr/tr/download/article-file/1911471

UN. (2020). *International Migration 2020.* Department of Economic and Social Affairs. Retrieved November 18, 2023, from https://www.un.org/development/desa/pd/sites/www.un.org.development.desa.pd/files/undesa_pd_2020_internatio nal_migration _highlights.pdf

UN. (2022a). *World population prospects.* Department of Economic and Social Affairs. Retrieved November 24, 2023, from https://population.un.org/wpp/

UN. (2022b). World Migration Report-2022. Interactive World Migration Report 2022 (iom.int). Retrieved November 23, 2023, from. https://digitallibrary.un.org/record/3951157?in=en.&v=pdf#files

UNESCO. (2016). *Who pays, for what, in education?* Institute for Statistics, Canada.

UNICEF. (2015). Education and equity. Retrieved November 15, 2023, from www.unicef.org/publications/files/

Winthrop, R., et al. (2023). *Investment in global education.* Brookings Institution. Investment-in-Global-Education-Final-web.pdf (brookings.edu). Retrieved November 20, 2023, from https://www.brookings.edu/wp-content/uploads/2016/06/Investment-in-Global-Education-Final-web.pdf

Wise, R. D. (2008). Migration and economic globalization: Introductory remarks. Retrieved March 31, 2025, from https://www.academia.edu/29037756/Migration_and_Economic_Globalization_Introductory_Remarks?auto=download&email_work_card=download-paper

World Bank. (2017). Migration and remittances, Factbook 2016. Retrieved May 30, 2017, from www.worldbank.org/en/topic/migrationremittancesdiasporaissue
World Development Report. (2023). Migrants, refugees and societies. Retrieved November 23, 2023, from https://openknowledge.worldbank.org/entities/publication/5e5ac9f1-71ee-4734-825e-60966658395f
World Population Review. (2020). Retrieved November 18, 2023, from https://worldpopulationreview.com/country-rankings/immigration-by-country

CHAPTER 2

On Causes and Costs of Brain Drain

Fikret Topal and *Zehra Hopyar*

Introduction

According to the International Organization for Migration (IOM), the global number of international migrants has been steadily increasing. In 1970, they were approximately 85 million international migrants, accounting for 2.3% of the world's population. By 2020, this figure had risen to 281 million, representing 3.6% of the global population. Over the span of half a century, the number of international migrants has grown by nearly 200 million. The majority are concentrated in Europe (87 million), Asia (86 million), and North America (59 million), collectively accounting for approximately 235 million migrants and forming the principal axis of global migration. While these figures may appear modest in relation to global population, they are significantly higher in certain countries. For

F. Topal (✉)
Department of Public Administration, Söke Faculty of Business, Adnan Menderes University, Aydın, Türkiye
e-mail: fikret.topal@adu.edu.tr

Z. Hopyar
Department of Sociology, Bursa Uludağ University, Bursa, Türkiye
e-mail: zhopyar@uludag.edu.tr

H. Gürak (ed.), *The Economics of Migration of Highly Skilled Workers from Türkiye*,
https://doi.org/10.1007/978-3-032-10606-3_2

instance, in the United Arab Emirates (UAE), international migrants constitute 88% of the total population (IOM, 2024).

Approximately 40% of all international migrants worldwide—around 115 million individuals—are of Asian origin, with India ranking as the leading country of origin both within Asia and globally. The top five countries with the highest number of international migrants worldwide are India, followed by Mexico, Russia, Syria, and China. In terms of destination, the United States (US) hosts the largest number of international migrants, with an estimated 51 million individuals. Germany follows with approximately 16 million and is succeeded by Saudi Arabia, Russia, and the United Kingdom (UK) (IOM, 2024). This data also highlights that global migration flows predominantly following east-west trajectory.

In the twenty-first century, the need for qualified people has increased day by day in the face of globalization, technological developments, and a transforming workforce. It has also become important for developed countries to attract qualified migrants. For developing countries, the loss of such migrants has been considered an important problem, as this type of migration mobility causes a serious shortage of trained human resources. The literature focusing on this type of mobility refers to different concepts to describe the situation. In this context, many concepts such as "human capital flight", "brain outflow", "intellectual migration", "scientific diaspora", "brain loss", "brain waste" (Durmaz, 2022), "talent drain" (Ndiangui, 2021), "brain gain", "brain circulation" (Teney, 2019), and "talent flow" (Carr et al., 2005) are used to express this phenomenon. Each concept has been coined by those who interpret the mobility of highly skilled individuals as a matter of gain, loss, both, or neither—each perspective carrying distinct implications. Some see this mobility as a gain while others see it as a loss for the sending country. Others refer to more comprehensive concepts outside of both. However, for a long time, the literature has been addressing this mobility from the perspective of developing countries and the discussion has surrounded the concept of "brain drain". As a matter of fact, this study addresses the issue from the perspective of Türkiye and reads or evaluates this phenomenon as brain drain.

The concept of brain drain refers to the migration of *highly skilled and educated people from developing countries to developed countries.* Education here is mainly centered on university education, where high qualifications are thought to be acquired. It is a conceptualization coined by the United Kingdom (UK) as a result of the migration of scientists and National Health Service (NHS) workers to North America for better opportunities and salaries. Brain drain refers to a more extreme and alarming level of migration beyond the normal migration of educated and qualified people (Johnson, 1965, p. 299). This process leads to further depletion of the already scarce human capital in underdeveloped countries, hindering economic growth and increasing welfare. Thus, both the resources spent on training qualified people and the loss of human capital required for economic growth create a lose-lose situation. Therefore, this situation is seen as a "drain" for the country that loses its educated workforce.

As mentioned, brain drain is seen as an important problem for developing countries. In this context, certain regions and countries around the world have become famous for brain drain. For example, while the African continent (especially South Africa and Sub-Saharan Africa) is known for the migration of healthcare workers (Dovlo, 2004; Mills et al., 2011; George et al., 2013; Capuano & Marfouk, 2013; Atte, 2021; Nwadiuko, 2021), engineering and IT workers migrate intensively in the Asian region (Jha et al., 2024). For example, over 2 million IT professionals have emigrated from India since the late 1990s (George, 2023, p. 22). Pakistan is also one of the countries suffering the most from brain drain, with around 600,000 highly qualified and highly skilled people leaving the country in the last 5 years (Khan, 2024, p. 387).

Today, brain drain is not only a major concern for developing countries but also becoming a problem for developed countries. For example, academics and researchers from Europe are moving to the US. The main dynamics of migration in this academic dimension include push factors such as low wages, job insecurity, and unfair recruitment processes, as well as pull factors such as attractive migration policies and the internationalization of education (Khan, 2021, pp. 266, 273).

While the issue of brain drain has become a global phenomenon, in recent years Türkiye has also become one of the countries experiencing significant emigration of highly skilled individuals. In fact, according to IOM data, Türkiye ranks 20th among the countries with the highest number of emigrants. The primary migration corridor from Türkiye is to Germany, followed by France, the Netherlands, Austria, and the US (IOM, 2024). Due to the increase in brain drain, especially since the 2010s, the Turkish public and academia have frequently addressed this issue. On the other hand, it is seen that policymakers have also put in place various strategies to prevent or reverse brain drain and have taken various steps in this context.[1] So, this study first analyzes the increasing brain drain in Türkiye in the post-2010 period and presents the relevant data. It then focuses on the causes and consequences of brain drain and discusses which motives are effective in brain drain and the cost of brain drain. The last section discusses the steps taken in the context of reverse migration in Türkiye.

Brain Drain of Highly Educated Individuals from Türkiye

The nature of migration from Türkiye, which started in the 1960s, has changed considerably over time. The period between 1960 and 1980, which was characterized by low-skilled and mostly labor migration (and related family reunification, marriage, etc.), has been replaced by high-skilled migration since the mid-2000s. Among the main reasons for this situation, it is possible to say that both global developments and local dynamics are effective. The innovations brought about by the transformation process in communication and information technologies in the world, especially after the 1990s, have changed the nature of the labor force need, while the transforming structural environment has now required a more qualified labor force. In addition, developments in Türkiye have also affected the quality of migrants as they have changed the quality of Türkiye's human capital. In this context, the increasing rate of tertiary education since the 2000s has played an important role. Thus, while the share of associate's, bachelor's, master's, and doctorate graduates in the population aged 25 and above (approximately 40 million) was 9.8% in 2008, the share of graduates in these groups in the population aged 25 and above (approximately 54 million) was 24.6% in 2023 (Turkish Statistical Institute-TurkStat, 2024a).

The emergence of qualified migration from Türkiye as a significant issue coincided with the years after 2010. In this context, it may be asserted

[1] As a result of concerns about the increasing brain drain, various policies have been implemented by the AK Party, which has been in government for many years. These include, for example, programs such as the "Reverse Brain Drain Program", "Leading Researchers Program", and "A National Leading Researchers Program" under TÜBİTAK (The Scientific and Technological Research Council of Türkiye), "TalentforBIZ" run by the Presidential Human Resources Office, and various scholarships and awards run by YTB (Presidency for Turks Abroad and Related Communities). For more details, see (Akyıldız, 2025) and section of the "Reversing The Brain Drain" in this chapter.

that qualified migration from Türkiye increased even more as a result of the socio-political developments in the post-2013 period. It is no coincidence that it was precisely during this period that a thread called "support platform for those who want to leave the country" was initiated on Ekşisözlük[2] (2025), a well-known social media platform. Under this heading, thousands of people exchanged ideas or gave advice and provided guidance to those who wanted to live abroad. Moreover, this thread is still being used effectively today.

Looking at the migration statistics of Turks between 2016 and 2023, it is seen that the number of departing Turks has increased even more, especially in recent years. In 2023, there is a difference of nearly 190,000 in this context (emigrants: 291,377 and immigrants: 101,677). It is an inevitable fact that as the number of departures increases, the number of qualified migrants also increases. Indeed, although it is not possible to see the current figures, the "Brain Drain Statistics" prepared by the TurkStat for the first time in 2024 show a rising trend. According to these figures, the rate, which was 1.6% in 2015, was 2.1% in 2022 and 2% in 2023. According to TurkStat methodology, it is necessary to wait until the 2030s to see the current rates (TurkStat, 2024b, see Graph 2.1).

In any case, the increase in the number of students attending universities mentioned earlier shows the seriousness of this proportional increase. A purely numerical look at these data shows that the increase is much higher. For example, according to data from the Council of Higher Education (YÖK), between 2000 and 2009, a total of 3,360,211 people graduated from university programs at the associate, bachelor's, master's, and doctoral levels. Among these, the number of bachelor's degree graduates is 1,930,790. In this case, the number of brain drain is approximately 31,000 people in 2015. Between 2008 and 2017, the number of all graduates at the same level was 6,401,700. Among these, the number of bachelor's degree graduates was 3,568,427. In this case, the number of brain drain for 2023 is approximately 72,000. In other words, there has been an increase of approximately 132%. Considering that almost half a million people graduate with a bachelor's degree every year in the Turkish university education system (and 3,025,0943 people have already graduated

[2] Ekşisözlük. (2025). Ülkeyi terk etmek isteyenlere destek platformu [Support platform for those who want to leave the country]. Ekşi Sözlük. https://eksisozluk.com/ulkeyi-terk-etmek-isteyenlere-destek-platformu%2D%2D4103378?p=99, Accessed at 2024.12.05.

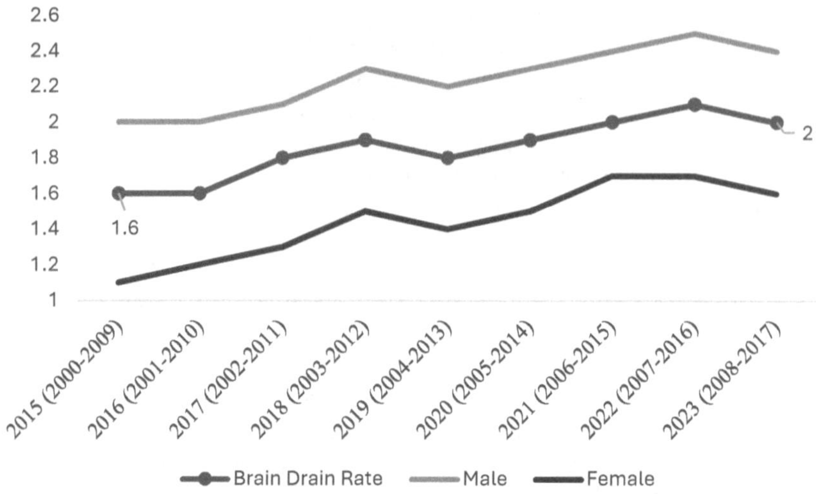

Graph 2.1 Brain drain rate of higher education graduates 2015–2023*. (Source: TurkStat. (2024b, September 26). Higher Education Brain Drain Statistics, 2021–2023. https://data.tuik.gov.tr/Bulten/Index?p=Higher-Education-Brain-Drain-Statistics-2021-2023-53839&dil=2#:~:text=Brain%20drain%20rate%20of%20higher,males%20is%202.4%25%20in%202023, Accessed at 2024.11.03. [*According to this calculation made by TurkStat, a range of 15 years to 6 years is taken into account for each reference year. Accordingly, for the data for 2023, it is necessary to have graduated from one of the undergraduate programs between 2008 and 2017. These graduates must have been abroad for at least 3 years between 2018 and 2022 and must definitely be abroad in the reference year (in this case 2023)]).

from a bachelor's degree program in the 2018–2023 period), the seriousness of the situation becomes clearer (YÖK, 2025).

European countries are largely among the first choices of skilled migrants. These countries are seen as attraction centers for skilled labor. In this context, the World Talent Index shows the success of European countries in attracting skilled people. Among the countries analyzed by this index, European states rank high with their competitive and attractive structure (IMD, 2024). Similarly, it is possible to say that Europe is one of the first destinations preferred by qualified migrants from Türkiye. In fact, TurkStat data also confirms this. In the data set prepared with reference to

2023, the top five are the US, Germany, the UK, the Netherlands and Canada, respectively (TurkStat, 2024c).

Both geographical proximity and historical ties (migrations, bilateral relations, trade, etc.) are among the main reasons for this preference, and the number of asylum seekers is increasing day by day. As of 2014, the number of first-time asylum applicants to European countries is even clearer. And 4715 first-time applicants in 2014 increased by nearly 20 times to 97,190 in 2023. As can be seen, the number of Turkish citizens applying for asylum in European countries is increasing day by day. In the last 10 years, approximately 275,000 people have applied for the first time, of which 192,850 (70%) were men and 81,190 (30%) were women (Eurostat, 2024).

Approximately 90% of all applications in this process are distributed among six countries. These countries are Germany, France, Switzerland, Greece, Austria, the Netherlands, and Belgium. In fact, approximately 190,000 of these applicants are between the ages of 0 and 34. Among these, 65,875 applicants are under the age of 18, while 123,390 are in the 18–34 age group. Both groups account for 76.5% of the total (Eurostat, 2024). Although we do not have clear data on the education level of those who go abroad, it would not be wrong to say that the majority of those leaving have a high level of education. According to statistics released by the German Federal Statistical Office, about half of the asylum seekers from Türkiye are university graduates (DW, 2019).

Especially in the last 10 years, professionals such as doctors, engineers, researchers and academics, and young people who have been going abroad since high school have been at the center of brain drain discussions. In this context, for example, according to data from the Turkish Medical Association, the "good standing certificate"[3] given to those who want to work abroad was 90 in 2013, 931 in 2020, and 3025 in 2023 (Turkish Medical Association, 2023). Hundreds of people working in important defense industry companies in Türkiye go abroad every year. The Netherlands ranks first among the countries where Turkish engineers migrate in terms of the defense industry. ASML (Advanced Semiconductor

[3] "certificate of good standing" is a document that is required by health institutions abroad at the application stage as a kind of clean paper showing the diploma and disciplinary record of doctors. Although we do not have any data on how many of those who have obtained this certificate have traveled abroad, the increasing number of applications is important in terms of showing that there is a preparation or trend in this direction. For more information see Chap. 3.

Materials Lithography), one of the leading companies in the Netherlands, employs 1300 Turkish engineers (Karaçay, 2024). In this regard, when we look at the answers of the respondents to the survey conducted by the Presidency of Defense Industry in 2018 for those who worked in the defense industry but left their jobs to go abroad, the top three preferred countries are the Netherlands, the US, and Germany (Independent, 2019). According to the data shared by the Dutch Migration and Citizenship Authority, the number of applications from qualified migrants is increasing day by day. From 540 in 2016, this number increased to 780 in 2017 and over a thousand in 2018 (Özkan, 2019).

It is clear that brain drain, which can be observed in almost every field, has been on the rise in recent years. For example, while the number of researchers per capita in Türkiye increased after the 1970s until 2015, the number of researchers started to decline after 2015. There has been an increase in the number of academics going abroad in the period after 2013. In fact, the number of academics going abroad doubled in 2016. Today, there are approximately 11,200 Turkish researchers abroad. Especially after these years, the possibility of researchers migrating abroad has increased significantly (Akçiğit et al., 2023, pp. 20, 29; TBV, n.d.).

Another worrying aspect of brain drain in Türkiye is that of those who want to leave but cannot. It is possible to observe an increase in the intention to migrate in many sectors or students. Such migrants are among the involuntary non-migrants (Carling & Schewel, 2018) and possible candidates for migration. According to a study, while the rate of those who were moderate to go abroad was 24% in 2010, this rate increased to 35% in 2020, and among this rate, young people increased from 28% in 2010 to 48% in 2020 (Ağırdır, 2022). It is possible to observe this trend in dozens of different qualified job fields. For example, according to a survey conducted with 1710 people in Istanbul for engineers, 25% of engineers want to go to a different country. Among these, the proportion of engineering students between the ages of 18 and 22 reaches 50% (TMMOB Chamber of Mechanical Engineers, 2024). Students studying at universities such as Boğaziçi, Middle East Technical University (METU), and Istanbul Technical University (ITU), which are preferred by Türkiye's most successful students, are also interested in going abroad. In a survey conducted with 165 students studying in the computer engineering departments of these three universities, 92% (152) of the respondents stated that they would like to go abroad. Of those who wanted to go abroad, 86% (130) stated that they would never want to return to Türkiye (Oksijen, 2022).

In 2023, Konrad Adenauer Stiftung (2023, p. 7) conducted a Türkiye-wide youth survey with 2140 people between the ages of 18 and 25, 63% of young people stated that they would like to live in another country if given the opportunity. The top five countries were Germany (14.5%), the US (13.8%), the UK (9.8%), Canada (7%), and Norway (6.7%).

Causes of Brain Drain of Highly Educated Individuals

The data shows that since the mid-2010s, there has been a gradual increase in mobility from Türkiye to abroad. What explains the onset of this increase after the mid-2010s? What motivation is brain drain taking place? What are the main dynamics that explain this increase? This chapter seeks answers to these questions and draws on the migration literature. Evaluations on the causes of brain drain are in close relation with the general migration literature.

Theories of international migration are used to classify the causes of brain drain. Among these theories, the prominent ones are mentioned in understanding brain drain. The first of these is the "push-pull" theory, which provides a simple understanding of all migration movements. A person makes the decision to migrate under the influence of push factors in one place and pull factors in a different place. As a result of most of the research, it has been observed that highly qualified individuals are "pushed" by negative factors in their home country and "pulled" by positive factors in other countries (Sağırlı, 2006, p. 58). Accordingly, while reasons such as unemployment, inflation, political instability, poor management performance, low quality of life and wages, lack of merit, discrimination are push factors, technological development, incentives for qualified labor force, giving importance to merit, better job opportunities, and living conditions can be considered as pull factors.

Brain drain can be shaped by individual/internal reasons, but it also corresponds to a process in which external influences are also in play. The "center of attraction approach" in this context is based on the attraction created by the high level of prosperity of certain countries on potential migrants. The opportunities that certain regions of the world have can make those regions attractive for qualified people (Erdoğan, 2003, p. 89). These opportunities are more directly and indirectly related to the high level of welfare. Another approach, the "network theory", focuses on the effects of individual ties between former migrants, migrants, and potential migrants in the source and destination countries on the migration process based on variables such as hometown, kinship, friendship, professional affinity. Through social networks, information on migration procedures, the process of finding financial support, job opportunities, accommodation, bureaucratic procedures, and psychological/spiritual support can be accessed (Meyer, 2001, p. 93). Rather than the reason for migration, the social networks of the individual can be effective in choosing the place and time of migration.

There is also a different understanding effort based on the "macro-meso-micro" distinction and prioritized by some researchers (Faist, 2000; Black, et al., 2011; Timmerman et al., 2014; Castelli, 2018; Toyin-Thomas et al., 2023). According to this distinction, social, political, economic, environmental, and demographic factors constitute macro factors. These are reasons that are seen as independent of individuals and affect everyone in society. However, in terms of their consequences, they do not produce the same result for each individual. The second distinction is meso factors, which are related to individuals, but not entirely dependent on them, and are more likely to be influenced by social networks and connections. The third distinction is micro factors, which are centered on more individual characteristics.

All these discussions lead us to the "structure-agent" debate, which is one of the fundamental debates of the discipline of sociology. This debate, which is used to explain social phenomena, has emerged from the question of which one is effective. The phenomenon of migration has often had its share of this debate and has been trapped in this dichotomy. However, according to the new approach that has become evident in recent years, it is more accurate to evaluate the migration phenomenon outside of this debate due to its complex, multi-layered, and dynamic structure (Bakewell, 2010). It is argued that in order to understand the phenomenon of migration, it is necessary to consider the impact of structures and individuals together and the importance of more pluralistic approaches that transcend the structure-agent dichotomy (Collinson, 2009; de Haas, 2010). The mobility of the migrant can be understood within the interrelationship of the opportunities opened or constraints caused by the structural factors in which the person is embedded (Danış, 2023, p. 18). Therefore, it is possible to say that many factors intertwined with economic, political, individual, or socio-cultural dynamics are effective in the migration process. This study approaches the causes of brain drain from this perspective and considers it as a phenomenon shaped by structural problems such as differences in the welfare level of countries, discrimination, political conflicts, and the individual preferences and expectations of individuals.

While some of the structural causes of brain drain are effective on a global scale, others are country specific. For example, violence in health is a global problem. The phenomenon of violence is prominent in the health sector and causes social, mental, and physical harm to health workers. According to the World Health Organization (WHO), approximately 62% of healthcare workers globally are exposed to violence in the workplace. Verbal abuse (58%) is the most common form of violence, followed by threats (33%) and harassment (12%) (WHO, 2024a). Increasing incidents of violence pose a risk to the quality of healthcare services worldwide and are cited as one of the main reasons for brain drain (Kabbash et al., 2021). Another study among nurses showed that more than half of them want to migrate to other countries due to lack of career opportunities, low wages, and unfavorable working conditions (Kadel & Bhandari, 2019). The literature indicates that the desire for an increase in income levels is a strong pull factor for migration tendencies in parallel with the increase in the education level and professional experience of healthcare professionals (Muula, 2005).

The situation in Türkiye regarding violence in the health sector does not seem to be very different from other countries. According to the reports of the Health and Social Service Employees Union, there were 190 incidents of violence in health in Türkiye in 2021, and 316 health workers were subjected to violence in 2022. In 249 cases of violence, 422 health workers were victims of violence (Sağlık-Sen, 2023). In addition to violence in the health sector, dissatisfaction with income and working conditions is also a factor in this new wave of brain drain, which has increased significantly in recent years and is also called the "migration of doctors and engineers". Some studies reveal that low income level is a determining dynamic in the attitudes of health workers toward brain drain; and that as the education level of health workers increases, their search for professional advancement, job security, and better working conditions also increases; and that these factors come together to strengthen individuals' brain drain tendencies (Özdemir & Korkutan, 2024; Giurgiuca et al., 2018). The results of the Ministry of Health 2024 3rd period initial and reappointment lottery once again confirm this situation. Of the 2685 specialist positions that were opened in the appointment lottery, 318 or only 12% were filled and none of the 34 out of 81 provinces were preferred.

These provinces are mainly located in eastern and southeastern Anatolia. The vacancies were mainly in the fields of pediatric emergency, pediatric surgery, pediatric gastroenterology and pediatric metabolic diseases (Bahçetepe, 2025).

The desire to migrate is seen not only in senior healthcare professionals but also in young people at the beginning of their healthcare careers. In various studies conducted with medical students and physician assistants in Türkiye, participants expressed their desire to work abroad due to problems in the health system and difficult living and working conditions. The main reasons for this desire were high income, better employment and living conditions, violence in health, and long working hours (Filiz et al., 2022; Sancak et al., 2023; Uğur, 2022). Medical faculty students think about working abroad when they are in the fifth and sixth grade. Among the main reasons for this idea are better living conditions, lifestyle and high living standards, professionally protective legal regulations, and economic reasons (Erdoğan Kaya et al., 2023, p. 528).

An important issue in brain drain is the value given to scientific activities. Countries that are progressing in R&D activities, which are constantly increasing in importance all over the world, are becoming attractive for qualified people. Between 2015 and 2019, Türkiye's share of R&D expenditures in gross domestic product was well behind that of other countries. While the OECD average was 2.31 in 2015, it was 0.87 in Türkiye, and while it was 2.47 in the OECD in 2019, it was 1.06 in Türkiye (OECD, 2021). Failure to allocate sufficient resources to research and development and to improve conditions may be among the reasons for potential qualified migrants to leave Türkiye.

In addition, political developments that pose security threats, such as terrorism, war, coup d'état, suppression of freedoms (religious, sexual, etc.), ethnic issues and socio-political developments, also play a major role in the migration process. For example, the main motivations of skilled migrants leaving Greece include socio-cultural crisis and high levels of political corruption (65%) and work-related issues (low wages, poor working conditions, low employment, and job insecurity) (35%) (Panagiotakopoulos, 2020). Security threats do not always mean armed conflict, and increased uncertainty due to social and political developments in the country and the deterioration of the economy are often felt as security threats by individuals. According to Babaeker-Şap, the reasons for brain drain from Türkiye include anxiety about the future (worries about finding a job), perception of corruption, lack of merit (worries about not being close to the government), feeling of worthlessness (the desire to live in a place where business is done by reason rather than living in a place where connections solve business), climate of fear (not being able to speak out, worries that speaking out will get you in trouble), concerns about education policies, the search for freedom, higher quality education, and a comfortable life (2019). The French News Agency's interviews with people who have left Türkiye and those who are considering leaving Türkiye suggest that there are three main reasons for this migration: declining job opportunities for university graduates, increasing conservatism, and declining human rights and freedoms (BBC, 2017).

In another study conducted on highly qualified individuals who emigrated from Türkiye, attractive factors such as institutionalized functioning, political freedoms, and education without exams ranked first among the reasons for brain drain compared to other attractive factors, while repulsive factors such as ethnic discrimination, distrust of the state, and unemployment also ranked first (Aytaç & Aydın, 2019, p.80). According to Konrad Adenauer Stiftung's research, better living conditions (47.8%), and more freedom (20.7%) were the main reasons why people want to live in another country (2023, p. 12). For Besim Dellaloğlu, well-known sociologist, some of the reasons for the brain drain, which has increased significantly in Türkiye in recent years, are attributed to the erosion of democratic norms. Dellaloğlu states that he does not believe that the direction of this migration will change without a decrease in polarization in Türkiye, that highly educated individuals from almost every sector are leaving Türkiye, although there is a visible increase in the medical and IT sectors, and that the economic crisis and increasing authoritarianism are the two main reasons for this migration (Badendieck, 2023). According to the results of the research examining the criteria affecting brain drain decisions, career and government are the most important clusters that play a role in making this decision: while political and economic situation and restriction of fundamental rights and freedoms are the most important criteria in the government cluster, career opportunities, working environment, and wage policy have the highest priorities in the career cluster (Incekas & Kadaifci, 2022). A study from 2020, economic and political reasons, insufficient job opportunities, limitations in education, and personal development were cited as the main reasons for qualified individuals' decisions to leave the country (Kuran, 2021, p. 48).

As can be seen, brain drain is shaped by reasons related to many structural and individual dynamics. Reasons that are prominent in a country at certain time intervals may lose their primacy when history changes and other reasons may become more important (Hopyar, 2024, p. 176). In this context, the main reasons for the brain drain in Türkiye in the last decade or so have been economic, political, and social factors. Accordingly, in Yalçınkaya and Dülger's classification, economic reasons are expressed as low salaries, wage differences between the private and public sectors, high taxes and unemployment, limited employment opportunities, the prevalence of the obligation to work in an unqualified or unqualified profession, and anxiety about the future. The intervention of politics in business life and its increasing influence on economic life are the main political factors. The desire to live in a country with a high level of welfare, the desire to have more social rights, and the desire to increase the living standards of family members are also among the social factors (2017, p. 1649)

Upon examining the relevant literature, it is observed that the primary theoretical framework shaping the emigration of highly skilled individuals from Türkiye is the *push-pull theory*. While alternative theoretical approaches may explain specific phases of the migration process, they are often insufficient to account for all the stages of this period in a comprehensive manner. When these push and pull factors are envisioned as points aligned along a single continuum, the factor that determines their nature—whether "push" or "pull"—is the lifestyle. Accordingly, the recent wave of brain drain from Türkiye can be directly classified as a form of lifestyle migration.

The main determinants of this process are push and pull factors associated with quality of life. These factors are shaped through the comparison of pre- and post-migration living conditions. As Benson and O'Reilly (2009a, 2009b) argue, lifestyle migration involves a deliberate effort to reorganize family, work, and personal priorities in order to pursue a more meaningful and fulfilling life. This type of migration includes both an "escape" from the constraints of the home country and the "construction of an alternative life" abroad.

In the Turkish context, the Gezi Park protests of 2013—considered a symbolic breaking point—marked the onset of this trend. Since then, various push factors have become increasingly prominent, including economic instability, political tensions, dissatisfaction with salaries, unemployment, and uncertainty about the future. On the other hand, pull factors such as freedom, a stronger welfare system, higher income satisfaction, better working conditions, and environmental quality have made life abroad more attractive for highly qualified individuals. For these reasons, this new wave of skilled emigration from Türkiye is increasingly conceptualized within the framework of lifestyle migration, shaped by the interplay of push and pull dynamics.

Costs of Brain Drain

As mentioned, brain drain generally refers to a flow from developing countries to developed countries. Indeed, among the largest migration corridors are routes to advanced economies such as the US, France, Russia, the UAE, and Saudi Arabia (IOM, 2024). Türkiye, in this context is also experiencing significant outflow of skilled labor toward developed countries. But what are the costs of this mobility for Türkiye?

Brain drain entails a range of economic costs, including the slowdown of economic growth, decline in national income, the expense of educating qualified individuals, reduction in tax revenues, and the contraction of circulation of knowledge, skills, and services (spillover effect). One of the most critical economic losses is the depletion of human capital—a form of long-term investment by the sending country. The departure of highly educated professionals not only leads to a direct loss of investment but also deprives institutions and the broader economy of productive capacity (Brock & Blake, 2015, p. 40).

Highly skilled migrants, in particular, carry higher economic value compared to unskilled migrants. While a skilled migrant is estimated to be worth around $100,000 in foreign direct investment, this figure drops to about $25,000 for an unskilled migrant (Bahar & Rapoport, 2018, p. 2). According to one study, "Türkiye's stock of migrants in 20 OECD countries amounts to $230 billion in outbound direct investment" (Aksoy, 2018). Although it is difficult to calculate exact economic losses, some estimations are revealing. For instance, the annual education cost for a single medical student is calculated at $21,832, amounting to approximately $130,000 over a six-year program (Abuhanoğlu et al., 2012, p. 62). Based on this estimate, the total education cost for all doctors who received a certificate of good conduct between 2013 and 2023 is around $1.5 billion.

Moreover, beyond the cost of formal education, the lifetime public investment in the form of subsidized health, justice, and communication services further increases the financial loss when these individuals emigrate post-graduation. These are opportunity costs for the sending country, which is effectively subsidizing the labor forces of wealthier nations.

The health sector provides a prominent example. The World Health Organization (WHO) reports a 60% increase in migrant doctors and nurses working in OECD countries between 2010 and 2020 (WHO, 2024b). Alongside its impact on public health systems, the migration of health workers imposes considerable financial costs on the country of origin due to its investment in medical education (Kamarulzaman et al., 2022). This is directly related to the third Sustainable Development Goal—"Healthy and Quality Life"—which calls for stronger recruitment and retention of health professionals, particularly in low- and middle-income countries (UN, 2024).

Similarly, the opportunity cost of brain drain is significant but often overlooked. In systems where education is publicly funded through taxes, the emigration of skilled individuals represents a lost opportunity to reap the return on investment domestically (Johnson, 1965, p. 302).

Although per-student expenditure in Türkiye's tertiary education has declined over the years, it still constitutes a significant financial burden—largely shouldered by the state. In 2023, 83.5% of per-student education expenditure was publicly funded (see Table 2.1).

Table 2.1 Tertiary education expenditure per student

Years	*Tertiary education expenditure per student ($)*
2013	6.380
2014	5.798
2015	4.574
2016	4.456
2017	3.736
2018	3.370
2019	3.314
2020	2.961
2021	3.223
2022	3.027
2023	3.563

Source: TurkStat. (2024d, December 5). Education expenditure statistics, 2023. https://data.tuik.gov.tr/Bulten/Index?p=Education-Expenditure-Statistics-2023-53557, Accessed at 2024.12.27

The migration of scientists and academics is particularly detrimental, given their central role in driving innovation and economic growth.[4] Studies show a strong correlation between national income and research outputs (Akçiğit et al., 2023). Türkiye lags behind OECD countries in both national income and the number of articles or patents per capita. The loss of highly trained researchers and innovators further restricts the country's ability to enhance its scientific and technological capacity.

Each case of skilled labor migration diminishes the country's potential productive capacity (Gürak, 2009, p. 126). Moreover, migration causes a loss of knowledge networks, depriving peers, students, and institutions of shared learning and collaboration opportunities (OECD, 2008, p. 70). Building human capital is a long-term investment—its loss is hard to replace.

In addition to economic concerns, brain drain also incurs social and political costs, including disruptions in family structures, educational discontinuity for children, and cultural adaptation challenges (OECD, 2008, p. 75). Nonetheless, these aspects are often overshadowed by economic debates.

It is worth acknowledging that brain drain may also yield potential benefits for sending countries. These include skill development among those preparing to migrate, diaspora networks, reverse migration of experienced professionals, and remittances (Brock & Blake, 2015, p.40). However, these gains are hard to quantify and vary greatly across contexts.

From an economic standpoint, remittances are frequently cited as a major benefit of migration. According to IOM (2024), global remittances reached $831 billion in 2022, with $647 billion flowing to low- and middle-income countries. Yet, Türkiye's share in global remittances has sharply declined since the early 2000s, now representing only 0.01% of GDP (World Bank, 2025). Moreover, research shows that remittances decrease as the migrant's education level increases (Niimi et al., 2010), which casts doubt on their role in compensating for the loss of high-skilled individuals.

[4] In the context of economic growth, the concepts of science and technology are frequently used interchangeably in the academic literature. However, several scholars contend that the primary requirement for countries such as Türkiye is not the proliferation of scientists but rather the development of engineers and technicians who possess the necessary expertise to effectively implement and utilize technological innovations (see Gürak, 2015, 2024).

Reversing the Brain Drain: Potential Remedy[5] for Reducing the Damage

Qualified migrants residing in developed countries represent a valuable opportunity for less developed nations to access highly skilled human resources in a relatively short time. Equipped with the knowledge and expertise gained abroad, these individuals can make significant contributions to the economic growth of their countries of origin—provided they are encouraged to return. This process of reverse brain drain can yield positive outcomes, especially if the institutional architecture in the home country offers adequate support and strategic direction (Gürak, 2024).

Türkiye has been implementing various policies and institutional arrangements in this regard to take measures against brain drain and reverse the process back. In order to prevent brain drain and increase the number of qualified labor force, various incentive programs have been implemented and policies including some legal regulations have been implemented in recent years. In this context, development plans, TOKTEN (The Transfer of Knowledge Through Expatriate Nationals) and TÜBİTAK programs, the Blue Card application, the efforts of the YTB, and the practices of private institutions stand out.

From the First Five-Year Development Plan covering the years 1963–1967 to the Twelfth Five-Year Development Plan covering the years 2024–2028, although Türkiye‘s migration movements are included in all development plans, there are no concrete policy recommendations for brain drain. For the first time in the Eleventh Five-Year Development Plan, it was mentioned that the causes of brain drain from Türkiye to abroad should be determined and research should be conducted to prevent brain drain and increase reverse brain drain (DPT, 2019, p. 133). The Twelfth Five-Year Development Plan, which is currently in force, states the following objectives: preventing the loss of qualified labor force, developing mechanisms to transfer professional knowledge and experience by strengthening the ties of qualified Turks abroad with the homeland, taking steps to prevent the mass loss of labor force on a sectoral basis by revealing the reasons for the migration of qualified labor force related to the labor market (DPT, 2023, p. 163). Although the existence of brain drain is mentioned in development plans, no concrete policy output has been put forward.

[5] We use this expression borrowed from Gürak's work. See more Gürak (2024).

TOKTEN is a program created by the United Nations Development Programme to promote reverse brain drain. One of the objectives of the program is to support the return of overseas experts from developing countries to their home countries to provide short-term technical assistance, thereby enabling them to use their knowledge and experience gained abroad to contribute to the development efforts of their countries. The first implementation of the program in Türkiye started at Karadeniz Technical University in 1977. As Kurtuluş states, with this project, experts served Türkiye in a total of 35 fields such as physics, mechanical, industrial, and metallurgical engineering, economics, marketing, computer sciences, etc., for periods ranging from 2 weeks to 12 weeks. The United Nations Development Organization, TÜBİTAK, and the State Planning Organization were also involved in the implementation of the program. By 1994, the number of beneficiaries of the program was 476 and in 1993, 77% of the beneficiaries were living in the US (Kurtuluş, 1999, pp. 117–119). Interest in this program waned over time.

Another Turkish practice to attract highly skilled foreign labor is the "Blue (Turquoise) Card", which entered into force in 2017. The background to the emergence of this card is the Tenth Development Plan and the Attraction Center for Skilled Manpower Program Action Plan. This card grants qualified foreigners the right to work and reside in Türkiye indefinitely and their relatives only the right to reside. The blue card is both a concrete step in brain drain policies and an important contribution to our fight against global competition. The first holder of the Turquoise Card was businessman Steven Young (Anadolu Agency, 2021).

At the meeting of the High Advisory Board chaired by President Recep Tayyip Erdoğan in 2020, the steps to be taken to encourage reverse brain drain were discussed, and it was stated that the steps to be taken to keep trained scientists in Türkiye and to ensure the return of those who went abroad were discussed and the possible contributions of the public and private sectors were also discussed (Demircan, 2020).

TÜBİTAK is one of the leading institutions in the development and support of science in Türkiye. In terms of brain drain, it also implements programs to encourage reverse brain drain. For many years, TÜBİTAK has organized various workshops under the name of "Research Destination Türkiye". Since 2010, a series of conferences titled "European and National Funding Opportunities for Brain Circulation" aimed to raise awareness for those who want to live in Türkiye again, reaching 500 highly qualified researchers in 12 different locations. Through the

European Union Marie Curie Actions and the European Research Council Program, 235 researchers were successfully reintegrated in Türkiye (TÜBİTAK, 2015).

TÜBİTAK's 2232 coded "International Leading Researchers Program" is one of the widely used programs for repatriation. The main purpose of this program is to enable researchers who want to share their experiences abroad with scientists in Türkiye to come to Türkiye. Universities, industrial organizations, and public institutions in Türkiye support these qualified researchers to come and contribute to our country. This 2232-coded program consists of "2232-A International Leading Researchers Program" and "2232-B International Young Researchers Program" (TÜBİTAK, 2024a). Minister of Industry and Technology Mustafa Varank announced in 2021 that the government will allocate up to 720,000 TL ($95,000) to researchers from abroad to conduct studies. It was stated that 243 applications were made to the International Leading Researchers Program run by TÜBİTAK and launched in 2018, 127 of which were selected and are conducting studies in different disciplines ranging from social sciences to health sciences (Daily Sabah, 2021). In the commercial shown by President Erdoğan ahead of the 2023 elections, the increase in the reverse mobility of the brain drain is underlined. In the video, Turkish scientists residing abroad are informed that under the "International Scholarship Program for Outstanding Researchers" launched in 2018, they will be provided with all the resources necessary to carry out their research if they return to their home country. It is also stated that, since 2018, approximately 6000 scientists have returned to Türkiye (Turkish Minute, 2023). Based on this public service announcement, the President encouraged the return of scientists who went abroad for better living conditions to Türkiye.

At the same time, according to the "Türkiye Academic Diaspora Report: From Brain Drain to Brain Power" prepared by the Turkish Informatics Foundation (TBV), there was a significant increase in the number of researchers per capita in Türkiye from the 1970s until 2015, but this increase reversed after 2015 and started to decline (Akçiğit et al., 2023). According to the results of the International Leading Researchers and International Young Researchers Programs in 2024, 40 researchers came to Türkiye and received support to start their projects (TÜBİTAK, 2024b). In addition to these, TÜBİTAK also has "2236 International Experienced Researcher Circulation Program" and "2221 Guest or Sabbatical Scientist Support Program" to attract qualified Turkish or foreign researchers from abroad. With this program, experienced researchers are supported to carry out their research projects in leading universities or industrial institutions and organizations in Türkiye (TÜBİTAK, 2024c). Technological developments in Türkiye are also followed by Turks living abroad. Gülin Dede, Coordinator of The European Space Research and Technology Centre (ESTEC), stated that Türkiye's space projects paved the way for reverse brain drain and proved the growth and success potential of the country's space sector, and expressed her desire to return to Türkiye to work and contribute to her country (Duyar, 2024).

There are also policies by private institutions to reverse the brain drain to Türkiye. Organizations such as Air Electronics Industry (HAVELSAN), Military Electronics Industry (ASELSAN), and Turkish Aerospace Industries (TAI) have initiated projects to encourage reverse brain drain. ASELSAN, which was established to meet the communication needs of the Turkish Armed Forces, emphasizes reverse brain drain in its recruitment processes. ASELSAN organizes career events at major universities around the world, conducts promotional activities in Silicon Valley, and participates in TÜBİTAK meetings. ASELSAN's "Back to Türkiye" project, which was launched in 2016, was renamed "Next Big Move to Türkiye" in 2020, and according to the statement made in 2021, 50 people have returned to Türkiye in the last 2 years within the scope of this project (Çetinkaya, 2021). HAVELSAN also stated that they are taking steps to bring qualified human resources who have gone abroad or are working abroad back to Türkiye and that 15 people working in important companies such as Google, Microsoft, Mastercard, and ASML have returned to Türkiye (Yıldırım, 2020). TAI, like others, is also calling for attracting highly qualified individuals to Türkiye through the "TAI reverse brain drain project" (TAI, 2024). The "A Ticket For Your Future" program launched by Arçelik aims to attract Turkish students studying abroad to work in Türkiye after graduation (Arçelik, 2024). Similarly, foundation universities have policies to support the arrival of academics from prestigious universities around the world in order to reverse the brain drain.

As can be seen, despite the completed and ongoing policies and practices, data on basic issues such as the number of returnees, the duration of their stay in Türkiye, and the sectors in which they work are very limited. While this lack of data constitutes a separate problem area, it seems that strategies to address the brain drain have not achieved sufficient success. There are studies claiming that the tendency of diaspora scientists to physically reverse the brain drain is low, whereas the tendency to intellectually contribute to Türkiye is quite high (Durmaz, 2022). Taking into account studies in the field and other experiences, Türkiye needs to transform its brain drain strategies.

Researchers with decreasing productivity abroad are more likely to return to Türkiye, while researchers with increasing productivity in Türkiye are more likely to move abroad. This means that the most productive researchers are brain drained. Those who return are among the less productive ones. As a matter of fact, the productivity of these researchers decreases even after they return to Türkiye. At this point, the structural environment in Türkiye (lack of research opportunities, high teaching load, etc.) also plays a role (Akçiğit et al., 2023, p. 33, 34). Patriotism, cultural images, or financial incentives are not enough to reverse brain drain. In order for returns to be permanent, dynamics such as physical facilities related to the workplace, the behavior of colleagues, and poorly defined duties and responsibilities may result in wasting the potential expected from reverse brain drain (Gürak, 2024, p. 417). Studies have been conducted on the problem areas and re-adaptation processes that qualified Turks face after returning to the country, and it has been seen that the reasons for their re-migration from Türkiye are related to these problem areas (Hopyar, 2023, pp. 167–189).

Conclusion

Since the mid-2010s, the number of expatriates in Türkiye has been increasing every day. The fact that most of the individuals emigrating from Türkiye are highly qualified young human resources between the ages of 25 and 35 means a significant loss of human capacity. While this trend is clearly observable in sectors such as medicine and engineering, it is also evident in other fields, where graduates of various universities—and even students from prestigious high schools—increasingly seek opportunities abroad. Among university graduates, there is a growing tendency to settle abroad following graduation, which signals a worrying loss of qualified human resources and poses long-term challenges for the country's development prospects.

It would not be inaccurate to assert that a combination of global developments and shifting domestic dynamics in Türkiye has facilitated the increasing outflow of skilled individuals. The primary drivers of this brain drain are economic challenges, closely intertwined with social and political factors. Among the most pressing concerns are the worsening economic conditions, inadequate salaries, and the significant decline in purchasing power. In addition, the quality and accessibility of education have emerged as major issues, particularly for families with children. Widespread perceptions of declining meritocracy and a persistently volatile political and social agenda further contribute to public disillusionment. These conditions have intensified feelings of uncertainty and anxiety among the younger population, fostering a sense of hopelessness and prompting many to seek alternative futures abroad.

Over the past decade, the issue of brain drain has gained significant prominence on Türkiye's national agenda. The gravity of the situation is underscored by indications that emigration is not a temporary trend but rather a long-term phenomenon that may intensify in the coming years. Empirical studies reveal a growing desire among various professional groups and students to seek opportunities abroad; however, many lack the necessary resources or conditions to do so. This has led to the emergence of a group often referred to as "involuntary non-migrants"—individuals who aspire to migrate but are constrained from doing so due to structural or financial barriers.

For many countries, preventing the emigration of highly qualified individuals has become a policy priority that often surpasses other migration-related concerns. Although efforts have been made to promote reverse brain drain, current initiatives appear insufficient, highlighting the need for more comprehensive and innovative strategies. While some measures have been introduced to address the economic concerns of potential returnees, these remain inadequate. Sustainable solutions must also aim to foster confidence in professional environments and ensure a sense of stability. Moreover, return incentive programs would benefit from incorporating mechanisms that support the social reintegration of returnees into life in Türkiye—particularly by promoting workplace environments grounded in meritocracy and psychological well-being.

References

Abuhanoğlu, H., Cankul, İ. H., & Ayanoğlu, Y. (2012). Mezuniyet öncesi tıp eğitimi maliyetlerinin belirlenmesi: Tıp fakültesinde bir uygulama [Determining the Cost of Undergraduate Medical Education: A Faculty of Medicine Aplication]. *Sağlıkta Performans ve Kalite Dergisi, 4*(2), 39–65.

Ağırdır, B. (2022, April 22). Bu topraklar göç coğrafyası [These lands are a migration geography]. *Oksijen*. Retrieved December 05, 2024, from https://gazeteoksijen.com/yazarlar/bekir-agirdir/bu-topraklar-goc-cografyasi-152906

Akçiğit, U., Koç, Ç., Parmar, S., Pearce, J., Saygın, Z. B., Shim, Y., Taşpınar, N., & Tokmakoğlu, D. (2023). *Türkiye akademik diaspora raporu: Beyin göçünden beyin gücüne* [Turkey academic diaspora report: From brain drain to brain power]. Türkiye Bilişim Vakfı.

Aksoy, M. (2018, November 2). Beyin göçünün önlenemez yükselişi [The unstoppable rise of brain drain]. *Bağımsız Gazetecilik Platformu*. Retrieved December 15, 2024, from https://platform24.org/beyin-gocunun-onlenemez-yukselisi/

Akyıldız, İ. E. (2025). Beyin Göçü Politikaları: Dünya'dan ve Türkiye'den Örnekler. *Anadolu Üniversitesi İktisadi ve İdari Bilimler Fakültesi Dergisi, 26*(1), 326–361. https://doi.org/10.53443/anadoluibfd.1531641

Anadolu Agency. (2021, September 10). Türkiye'de yabancı girişimciye Turkuaz Kart uygulaması başladı [*Turquoise Card system launched in Turkey for foreign entrepreneurs]*. Anadolu Agency. Retrieved December 14, 2024, from https://www.aa.com.tr/en/economy/turquoise-card-system-launched-in-turkey-for-foreign-entrepreneurs/2367091

Arçelik. (2024). *A ticket for your future programının 2'nci etabı için başvuru süreci başladı* [The application process for the second phase of the 'A Ticket for Your Future' program has begun]. Retrieved December 15, 2024, from https://www.arcelikglobal.com/tr/sirket/medya/basin-bultenleri/a-ticket-for-your-future-programinin-2nci-etabi-icin-basvuru-sureci-basladi/

Atte, F. (2021). The moral challenges of health care providers brain drain phenomenon. *Public Policy and Law, 16*(2), 67–73. https://doi.org/10.1177/1477750920946614

Aytaç, S., & Aydın, G. Ç. (2019). Analysis of the effects of pull and push factors on brain drain: An example of Turkey. *Journal of Social Economics Research, 6*(2), 74–84. https://doi.org/10.18488/journal.35.2019.62.74.84

Babaeker-Şap, B. (2019, April 23). Bir beka sorunu olarak beyin göçü… Türkiye "aklını" neden kaybediyor? Gidenler ve gitmek için uğraşanlar anlattı [Brain drain as a survival issue… Why is Turkey losing its "mind"? Those who left and those trying to leave tell their stories]. *Indy Türk*. Retrieved December 13, 2024, from https://www.indyturk.com/node/24501/haber/bir-beka-sorunu-olarak-beyin-#google_vignette

Badendieck, R. (2023, October 29). Turkey is marking its centennial. But a brain drain has cast a shadow on the occasion. *Independent*. Retrieved November 23, 2024, from https://www.independent.co.uk/news/turkey-ap-recep-tayyip-erdogan-germany-istanbul-b2444284.html

Bahar, D., & Rapoport, H. (2018). Migration, knowledge diffusion and the comparative advantage of nations. *The Economic Journal, 128*(612), F273–F305. https://doi.org/10.1111/ecoj.12450

Bahçetepe, S. (2025, January 08). 34 ilde tercih sayısı sıfır [Zero preferences in 34 provinces]. *Birgün*. Retrieved January 15, 2025, from https://www.birgun.net/haber/34-ilde-tercih-sayisi-sifir-589239

Bakewell, O. (2010). Some reflections on structure and agency in migration theory. *Journal of Ethnic and Migration Studies, 36*(10), 1689–1708. https://doi.org/10.1080/1369183X.2010.489382

BBC. (2017, September 11). AFP: Eğitimli gençler Türkiye'yi terk ediyor [AFP: Educated youth are leaving Turkey]. *BBC Türkçe*. Retrieved September 25, 2024, from https://www.bbc.com/turkce/haberler-turkiye-41331921

Benson, M., & O'Reilly, K. (2009a). Lifestyle migration: Escaping to the good life. In M. Benson & K. O'Reilly (Eds.), *Lifestyle migration: Expectations, aspirations and experiences* (pp. 1–14). Ashgate Publishing.

Benson, M., & O'Reilly, K. (2009b). Migration and the search for a better way of life: A critical exploration of lifestyle migration. *The Sociological Review, 57*(4), 608–625. https://doi.org/10.1111/j.1467-954X.2009.01864.x

Black, R., Adger, W. N., Arnell, N. W., Dercon, S., Geddes, A., & Thomas, D. (2011). The effect of environmental change on human migration. *Global Environmental Change, 21*(Supplement 1), 3–11. https://doi.org/10.1016/j.gloenvcha.2011.10.001

Brock, G., & Blake, M. (2015). *Debating brain drain: May governments restrict emigration?* Oxford University Press.

Capuano, S., & Marfouk, A. (2013). African brain drain and its impact on source countries: What do we know and what do we need to know? *Journal of Comparative Policy Analysis: Research and Practice, 15*(4), 297–314. https://doi.org/10.1080/13876988.2013.813122

Carling, J., & Schewel, K. (2018). Revisiting aspiration and ability in international migration. *Journal of Ethnic and Migration Studies, 44*(6), 945–963. https://doi.org/10.1080/1369183X.2017.1384146

Carr, S. C., Inkson, K., & Thorn, K. (2005). From global careers to talent flow: Reinterpreting "brain drain". *Journal of World Business, 40*(4), 386–398. https://doi.org/10.1016/j.jwb.2005.08.006

Castelli, F. (2018). Drivers of migration: Why do people move? *Journal of Travel Medicine, 25*(1), tay040. https://doi.org/10.1093/jtm/tay040

Çetinkaya, Z. (2021, March 10). ASELSAN, son iki yılda 50 yeteneği yurda döndürdü [ASELSAN brought back 50 talents in the last two years]. *Anadolu Agency*. Retrieved November 07, 2024, from https://www.aa.com.tr/tr/turkiye/aselsan-son-iki-yilda-50-yetenegi-yurda-dondurdu/2156407

Collinson, S. (2009). *The political economy of migration processes: An agenda for migration research and analysis*. IMI Working Papers, 12.

Daily Sabah. (2021, March 17). Turkey seeks to reverse brain drain with generous research grants. *Daily Sabah*. Retrieved November 05, 2024, from https://www.dailysabah.com/turkey/education/turkey-seeks-to-reverse-brain-drain-with-generous-research-grants

Danış, D. (2023). Günümüz Türkiye'sinde Beyin Göçü. In D. Danış (Ed.), *Gitmek ve Dönmek Arasında: Türkiye'de Yeni Nesil Beyin Göçü [Brain drain in contemporary Turkey, between leaving and returning: New generation brain drain in Turkey]* (pp. 9–28). Nika Yayınları.

De Haas, H. (2010). Migration and development: A theoretical perspective. *International Migration Review, 44*(1), 227–264. https://doi.org/10.1111/j.1747-7379.2009.00804.x

Demircan, F. (2020, February 5). Turkey's officials hold meeting to reverse brain drain. *Anadolu Agency*. Retrieved November 09, 2024, from https://www.aa.com.tr/en/turkey/turkeys-officials-hold-meeting-to-reverse-brain-drain/1736840

Dovlo, D. (2004). The brain drain in Africa: An emerging challenge to health professionals' education. *Journal of Higher Education in Africa / Revue de l'enseignement Supérieur en Afrique, 2*(3), 1–18. Retrieved December 05, 2024, from http://www.jstor.org/stable/24486291

DPT. (2019). *On birinci beş yıllık kalkınma planı* [Eleventh five-year development plan]. Retrieved December 05, 2024, from https://www.sbb.gov.tr/wp-content/uploads/2022/07/On_Birinci_Kalkinma_Plani-2019-2023.pdf

DPT. (2023). *On ikinci beş yıllık kalkınma planı* [Twelfth five-year development plan]. Retrieved December 05, 2024, from https://www.sbb.gov.tr/wp-content/uploads/2023/12/On-Ikinci-Kalkinma-Plani_2024-2028_11122023.pdf

Durmaz, A. (2022). Diaspora as a source of human capital: The effects of the relationship between scientific Turkish diaspora and the homeland on reverse brain drain. *Migration and Development, 11*(3), 717–736. https://doi.org/10.1080/21632324.2021.1959409

Duyar, Z. (2024, January 15). Türkiye's space projects facilitate reverse brain drain: Expert. *Anadolu Agency*. Retrieved December 15, 2024, from https://www.aa.com.tr/en/science-technology/turkiye-s-space-projects-facilitate-reverse-brain-drain-expert/3233593

DW. (2019, February 7). Almanya'ya iltica başvurularında Türkler Kürtleri geçti [Turks surpass Kurds in asylum applications to Germany]. *Deutsche Welle*. Retrieved September 25, 2024, from https://www.dw.com/tr/almanyaya-iltica-başvurularında-türkler-kürtleri-geçti/a-47402058

Ekşisözlük. (2025). Ülkeyi terk etmek isteyenlere destek platformu [Support platform for those who want to leave the country]. *Ekşi Sözlük*. Retrieved December 05, 2024, from https://eksisozluk.com/ulkeyi-terk-etmek-isteyenlere-destek-platformu%2D%2D4103378?p=99

Erdoğan, İ. (2003). Beyin göçü ve Türkiye [Brain drain and Turkey]. *Kuram ve Uygulamada Eğitim Bilimleri, 3*(1), 85–100.

Erdoğan, R. T. (2023). Beyin göçünü tersine çevirmeye devam edeceğiz [We will continue to reverse brain drain]. [Video]. YouTube. Retrieved December 15, 2024, from https://www.youtube.com/watch?v=oE7DRIvkbs0

Erdoğan Kaya, A., Erdoğan Aktürk, B., & Aslan, E. (2023). Factors predicting the motivation to study abroad in Turkish medical students: A causal investigation into the problem of brain drain. *Journal of Health Sciences and Medicine, 6*(2), 526–531. https://doi.org/10.32322/jhsm.1247070

Eurostat. (2024). Asylum applicants by type, citizenship, age and sex—Annual aggregated data. (Data extracted on September 15, 2024). *Eurostat*. Retrieved October 15, 2024, from https://ec.europa.eu/eurostat/databrowser/view/migr_asyappctza__custom_12876781/bookmark/table?lang=en&bookmarkId=0e0c6a6d-b3e0-4162-b23a-b65c4eff7a78

Faist, T. (2000). *The volume and dynamics of international migration and transnational social spaces*. Oxford University Press.

Filiz, M., Karagöz, M. B., & Karagöz, N. (2022). Tıp fakültesi öğrencilerinin beyin göçüne yönelik tutumlarının değerlendirilmesi [Evaluation of medical students' attitudes towards brain drain]. *Karadeniz Sosyal Bilimler Dergisi, 14*(27), 679–692. https://doi.org/10.38155/ksbd.1171838

George, A. S. (2023). Brain drain or brain gain: Assessing the costs and benefits of India's manpower exports. *Partners Universal International Innovation Journal (PUIIJ), 1*(6), 19–37. https://doi.org/10.5281/zenodo.10257669

George, G., Atujuna, M., & Gow, J. (2013). Migration of South African health workers: The extent to which financial considerations influence internal flows and external movements. *BMC Health Services Research, 13*(1), 297. https://doi.org/10.1186/1472-6963-13-297

Giurgiuca, A., Rosca, A. E., Matei, V. P., Gurgi-Oonvu, C., Zgarbura, R., Szalontay, A. S., & Pinto Da Costa, M. (2018). European Union mobility, income and brain drain: The attitudes towards migration of Romanian psychiatric trainees. *Review of Research and Social Intervention, 63*, 268–278.

Gürak, H. (2009). Küreselleşme ve doğrudan yabancı yatırımlar. In H. Gürak (Ed.), *Küreselleşme: Prof. Dr. Ayşe İrmiş'in katkılarıyla* (pp. 29–46) [e-kitap]. Retrieved February 15, 2025, from https://www.academia.edu/29706776/KÜRESELLEŞME_Prof_Dr_Ayşe_İrmişin_katkılarıyla

Gürak, H. (2015). *Economic growth and development: Theories, criticisms and an alternative growth model*. Peter Lang.

Gürak, H. (2024). Plundering the skilled workforce: Depriving developing nations of their most valuable assets, *World Review of Political Economy*, 15 (3), 406-421. Retrieved February 17, 2025, from https://www.jstor.org/stable/48812984

Hopyar, Z. (2023). *Almanya'dan Türkiye'ye nitelikli geriye göç hareketi: Karar verme ve yeniden uyum süreçleri* [Qualified return migration from Germany to

Turkey: Decision-making and reintegration processes] [Unpublished doctoral dissertation]. Sakarya University.

Hopyar, Z. (2024). Beyin göçünün yüz yılı: Türkiye'den dünyaya gidenler ve kalanlar [A century of brain drain: Those who left Turkey and those who stayed]. In F. Yaman (Ed.), *Türkiye'nin yüz yılı: Göç [Turkey's century: Migration]* (pp. 147–187). Nokta Yayınevi.

IMD (Institute for Management Development) (2024). IMD World Talent Ranking 2024: *The Socio-Economic Implications of AI in the Workplace*. Retrieved November 12, 2024, from https://www.imd.org/centers/wcc/worldcompetitiveness-center/rankings/world-talent-ranking/

İncekas, A. B., & Kadaifci, C. (2022). Brain drain: A multi-criteria decision model. In F. Calisir (Ed.), *Industrial engineering in the Internet-of-Things world* (pp. 271–282). Springer. https://doi.org/10.1007/978-3-030-76724-2_19

Independent. (2019, May 19). ASELSAN mühendisleri neden yurtdışına gidiyor, 'dönmek istiyorum' diyen çoğunluk neyi bekliyor? [Why are ASELSAN engineers going abroad, and what are the majority who say 'I want to return' waiting for?]. *Indy Türk*. Retrieved December 17, 2024, from https://www.indyturk.com/node/14551/haber/devlet-aselsan-roketsan-gibi-kritik-kurumlardan-ayrılıp-yurtdışına-giden

IOM (International Organization for Migration). (2024). *Interactive World Migration Report 2024*. Retrieved December 17, 2024, from https://worldmigrationreport.iom.int/msite/wmr-2024-interactive/

Jha, B. K., Thakur, R., Nepal, A., Chhetri, S., & Bhandary, B. (2024). Unraveling the brain drain dilemma: Analysis among skilled information technology professionals of Nepal. *Apex Journal of Business and Management, 2*(1), 127–138. https://doi.org/10.61274/apxc.2024.v02i01.010

Johnson, H. G. (1965). The economics of the "brain drain": The Canadian case. *Minerva, 3*(3), 299–311.

Kabbash, İ., El-Sallamy, R., Zayed, H., Alkhyate, İ., Omar, A., & Abdo, S. (2021). The brain drain: Why medical students and young physicians want to leave Egypt. *Eastern Mediterranean Health Journal, 27*(11), 1102–1108. https://doi.org/10.26719/emhj.21.066

Kadel, M., & Bhandari, M. (2019). Factors intended to brain drain among nurses working at private hospitals of Biratnagar, Nepal. *Bibechana, 16*, 213–220. https://doi.org/10.3126/bibechana.v16i0.21557

Kamarulzaman, A., Ramnarayan, K., & Mocumbi, A. O. (2022). Plugging the medical brain drain. *The Lancet, 400*(10366), 1492–1494. https://doi.org/10.1016/S0140-6736(22)01860-6

Karaçay, İ. (2024). Türkiye'den Hollanda'ya beyin göçü durmuyor [Brain drain from Turkey to the Netherlands continues]. *İlhan Karaçay*. Retrieved November 03, 2024, from https://www.ilhankaracay.com/turkiyeden-hollandaya-beyin-gocu-durmuyor/

Khan, J. (2021). European academic brain drain: A meta-synthesis. *European Journal of Education, 56*(2), 265–278. https://doi.org/10.1111/ejed.12448

Khan, A. M. (2024). The effect of brain drain on the economic growth of developing countries: Evidence from Pakistan. *Annals of Human and Social Sciences, 5*(2), 383–392.

Konrad Adenauer Stiftung. (2023). *Turkish youth study 2023.* Retrieved December 10, 2024, from https://www.kas.de/documents/283907/24685727/Turkish+Youth+Study+2023+Executive+Summary.pdf/0bd0a46d-c9ed-959c-5297-20e3a5355530?version=1.1&t=1685717331875

Kuran, E. (2021). *Onlar göçtü buradan, Türkiye'nin yeni göç nesli* [They migrated from here: Turkey's new migration generation]. Mundi Kitap.

Kurtuluş, B. (1999). *Amerika Birleşik Devletleri'ne Türk beyin göçü* [Turkish brain drain to the United States]. Aktüel Kitapevleri.

Meyer, J. B. (2001). Network approach versus brain drain: Lessons from the diaspora. *International Migration, 39*(5), 91–110. https://doi.org/10.1111/1468-2435.00173

Mills, E. J., Kanters, S., Hagopian, A., Bansback, N., Nachega, J., Alberton, M., Au-Yeung, C. G., Mtambo, A., Bourgeault, I. L., Luboga, S., Hogg, R. S., & Ford, N. (2011). The financial cost of doctors emigrating from sub-Saharan Africa: Human capital analysis. *BMJ, 343*, d7031. https://doi.org/10.1136/bmj.d7031

Muula, A. S. (2005). Is there any solution to the 'brain drain' of health professionals and knowledge from Africa? *Croatian Medical Journal, 46*(1), 21–29.

Ndiangui, P. (2021). From brain drain to brain gain: The battle against talent drain. *Journal of Culture and Values in Education, 4*(1), 34–48. https://doi.org/10.46303/jcve.2020.5

Niimi, Y., Ozden, C., & Schiff, M. (2010). Remittances and the brain drain: Skilled migrants do remit less. *Annals of Economics and Statistics, 97*(*98*), 123–141. https://doi.org/10.2307/41219112

Nwadiuko, J., Switzer, G. E., Stern, J., Day, C., & Paina, L. (2021). South African physician emigration and return migration, 1991–2017: A trend analysis. *Health Policy and Planning, 36*(5), 630–638. https://doi.org/10.1093/heapol/czaa193

OECD. (2008). The brain drain and negative social effects: When is the home country hurt? In *Policy coherence for development 2007: Migration and developing countries.* OECD Publishing. https://doi.org/10.1787/9789264027898-7-en

OECD. (2021). *Gross domestic spending on R&D* (indicator). Retrieved December 01, 2024, from https://www.oecd.org/en/data/indicators/gross-domestic-spending-on-r-d.html

Oksijen. (2022, January 7). En parlak gençlerimiz gidecek, bir daha geri gelmeyecek [Our brightest youth will leave and never return]. *Oksijen.* Retrieved

December 07, 2024, from https://gazeteoksijen.com/turkiye/en-parlak-genclerimiz-gidecek-bir-daha-geri-gelmeyecek-64627

Özdemir, N. E., & Korkutan, M. (2024). Türkiye'den Avrupa Ülkelerine Yönelik Sosyal Refah Göçü Üzerine Bir Değerlendirme. *Mavi Atlas, 12*(2), 280–294. https://doi.org/10.18795/gumusmaviatlas.1476858

Özkan, Y. (2019, January 6). Geçen yıl Türkiye'den 1020 kişi 'beyin göçü' için Hollanda'ya başvurdu [Last year, 1,020 people applied to the Netherlands for 'brain drain' from Turkey]. *BBC Türkçe.* Retrieved December 07, 2024, from https://www.bbc.com/turkce/haberler-dunya-46774679

Panagiotakopoulos, A. (2020). Investigating the factors affecting brain drain in Greece: Looking beyond the obvious. *World Journal of Entrepreneurship, Management and Sustainable Development, 16*(3), 207–218. https://doi.org/10.1108/WJEMSD-10-2019-0076

Sağırlı, M. (2006). *Eğitim ve insan kaynağı yönünden Türk beyin göçü: Geri dönen Türk akademisyenler üzerine alan araştırması* [Turkish brain drain in terms of education and human resources: A field study on returning Turkish academics] [Unpublished doctoral dissertation]. Istanbul University, Institute of Social Sciences.

Sağlık-Sen. (2023). *Sağlık-Sen 2022 yılı sağlıkta şiddet raporu* [Sağlık-Sen 2022 report on violence in healthcare]. Retrieved December 17, 2024, from https://www.sagliksen.org.tr/haber/12308/sagliksen.org.tr

Sancak, B., Selek, S. N., & Sarı, E. (2023). Depression, anxiety, stress levels and five-factor personality traits as predictors of clinical medical students' migration intention: A cross-sectional study of brain drain. *International Journal of Health Planning and Management, 38*(4), 1015–1031. https://doi.org/10.1002/hpm.3645

TAI (Turkish Aerospace Industries). (2024). *Tersine beyin göçü* [Reverse brain drain]. Retrieved November 03, 2024, from https://kariyer.tusas.com/tersine-beyin-gocu

TBV (Turkish Informatics Foundation). (n.d.). Beyin göçünden beyin gücüne! [From brain drain to brain power!]. Retrieved November 05, 2024, from https://tbv.org.tr/basin/beyin-gocunden-beyin-gucune

Teney, C. (2019). Immigration of highly skilled European professionals to Germany: Intra-EU brain gain or brain circulation? *Innovation: The European Journal of Social Science Research, 34*(1), 69–92. https://doi.org/10.1080/13511610.2019.1578197

Timmerman, C., Hemmerechts, K., & Marie-Lou De Clerck, H. (2014). The Relevance of a "Culture of Migration" in Understanding Migration Aspirations in Contemporary Turkey. *Turkish Studies, 15*(3), 496–518. https://doi.org/10.1080/14683849.2014.954748

TMMOB Chamber of Mechanical Engineers. (2024). *İstanbul'da yaşayan mühendisler araştırması 2024* [2024 survey of engineers living in Istanbul].

Retrieved October 09, 2024, from https://makina.mmo.org.tr/IstanbuldaYasayanMuhendislerArastirmasi

Toyin-Thomas, P., Ikhurionan, P., Omoyibo, E. E., et al. (2023). Drivers of health workers' migration, intention to migrate and non-migration from low/middle-income countries, 1970–2022: A systematic review. *BMJ Global Health, 8*(e012338), 1–12. https://doi.org/10.1136/bmjgh-2023-012338

TÜBİTAK (Scientific and Technological Research Council of Turkey). (2015). *TÜBİTAK reverse brain drain programme met with success.* Retrieved December 09, 2024, from https://tubitak.gov.tr/en/news/tubitak-reverse-brain-drain-programme-met-success

TÜBİTAK (Scientific and Technological Research Council of Turkey). (2024a). *2232 Uluslararası lider araştırmacılar programı* [2232 International leading researchers program]. Retrieved October 13, 2024, from https://tubitak.gov.tr/tr/burslar/uluslararasi/arastirma-burs-programlari/2232-uluslararasi-lider-arastirmacilar-programi

TÜBİTAK (Scientific and Technological Research Council of Turkey). (2024b). *2232-A Uluslararası lider araştırmacılar programı ve 2232-B Uluslararası genç araştırmacılar programı 2024 yılı 1. dönem başvuru sonuçları açıklandı* [Results of the 2024 first-term applications for the 2232-A International leading researchers program and 2232-B International young researchers program announced]. Retrieved October 13, 2024, from https://tubitak.gov.tr/tr/duyuru/2232-uluslararasi-lider-arastirmacilar-programi-ve-2232-b-uluslararasi-genc-arastirmacilar-programi-2024-yili-1-donem-basvuru-sonuclari-aciklandi

TÜBİTAK (Scientific and Technological Research Council of Turkey). (2024c). *2236 Uluslararası deneyimli araştırmacı dolaşımı destek programı* [2236 International experienced researcher circulation support program]. Retrieved October 13, 2024, from https://tubitak.gov.tr/tr/burslar/doktora-sonrasi/arastirma-burs-programlari/2236-uluslararasi-deneyimli-arastirmaci-dolasimi-destek-programi

Türk Tabipler Birliği [Turkish Medical Association]. (2023, December 29). *TTB'ye "İyi Hal Belgesi" başvuru sayısı* [Number of applications for "Good Conduct Certificates' to TTB] [Post on X]. X. Retrieved October 9, 2024, from https://x.com/ttborgtr/status/1740746140457279822

Turkish Minute. (2023, May 2). Erdoğan seeks to reverse brain drain from Turkey in public service announcement. *Turkish Minute.* Retrieved October 19, 2024, from https://turkishminute.com/2023/05/02/erdogan-seek-reverse-brain-drain-from-turkey-in-public-service-announcement/

TurkStat (Turkish Statistical Institute). (2024a, May 30). National education statistics 2023. Retrieved October 5, 2024, from https://data.tuik.gov.tr/Bulten/Index?p=Ulusal-Egitim-Istatistikleri-2023-53444

TurkStat (Turkish Statistical Institute). (2024b, September 26). Higher Education Brain Drain Statistics, 2021–2023. Retrieved November 03, 2024, from https://data.tuik.gov.tr/Bulten/Index?p=Higher-Education-Brain-Drain-Statistics-2021-2023-53839&dil=2#:~:text=Brain%20drain%20rate%20of%20higher,males%20is%202.4%25%20in%202023

TurkStat (Turkish Statistical Institute). (2024c, July 19). International migration statistics, 2023 (Migration to and from Turkey by citizenship country). Retrieved September 12, 2024, from https://data.tuik.gov.tr/Bulten/Index?p=Uluslararasi-Goc-Istatistikleri-2023-53544

TurkStat (Turkish Statistical Institute). (2024d, December 5). Education expenditure statistics, 2023. Retrieved December 29, 2024, from https://data.tuik.gov.tr/Bulten/Index?p=Education-Expenditure-Statistics-2023-53557

Uğur, N. (2022). Great risk for education cost: Brain drain (Resident physicians case). *Journal of Continuing Medical Education, 31*, 115–125.

UN (United Nations). (2024). *Department of Economic and Social Affairs, Sustainable Development.* Retrieved October 14, 2024, from https://sdgs.un.org/goals/goal3#targets_and_indicators

WHO (World Health Organization). (2024a). *Violence and harassment.* Retrieved September 10, 2024, from https://www.who.int/tools/occupational-hazards-in-health- sector/violence-harassment

WHO (World Health Organization). (2024b). *Health workforce—Migration.* Retrieved September 10, 2024, from https://www.who.int/teams/health-workforce/migration

World Bank. 2025 . *Personal remittances, received (% of GDP)—Turkiye.* Retrieved September 19, 2024, from https://data.worldbank.org/indicator/BX.TRF.PWKR.DT.GD.ZS?locations=TR&most_recent_value_desc=true

Yalçınkaya, H., & Dülger, S. (2017). Küreselleşmenin beyin göçü üzerindeki etkisi: Türkiye [The impact of globalization on brain drain: Turkey]. *International Journal of Social Humanities Sciences Research, 4*(14), 1646–1654.

Yıldırım, G. (2020, February 5). Dünya devlerinden ayrılıp Türkiye'ye döndüler [They left world giants and returned to Turkey]. *Anadolu Agency.* Retrieved September 09, 2024, from https://www.aa.com.tr/tr/ekonomi/dunya-devlerinden-ayrilip-turkiyeye-donduler/1736150

YÖK [Council of Higher Education]. (2025). *Yükseköğretim istatistikleri* [Higher education statistics]. Retrieved October 11, 2024, from https://istatistik.yok.gov.tr

CHAPTER 3

The Migration of Turkish Health Professionals: Causes and Consequences

Soner Tauscher and *Yigit Cem Eskicioglu*

Introduction

This study focuses exclusively on brain-drain involving **highly educated individuals**, with particular attention to the **implications** and **consequences** of their international migration for both sending and receiving countries. **Brain-drain** is the term used to describe the migration of educated and highly skilled individuals from one country to another, resulting in a loss of **Human Capital**[1] (HC) in one country or a gain for another. This phenomenon, which is usually discussed in terms of its economic and

[1] The term human capital is conceptualized as a key asset for the economic growth of countries, encompassing the knowledge and skills of highly educated individuals. It refers to the accumulation of expertise and competencies resulting from the migration of highly qualified professionals such as scientists, physicians, and engineers (Durmaz, 2022).

S. Tauscher (✉) • Y. C. Eskicioglu
Department of International Relations, Center for Diaspora Studies,
Sakarya University, Sakarya, Türkiye
e-mail: sonert@sakarya.edu.tr; yigiteskicioglu@sakarya.edu.tr

H. Gürak (ed.), *The Economics of Migration of Highly Skilled Workers from Türkiye*,
https://doi.org/10.1007/978-3-032-10606-3_3

social aspects, has led developed countries (DCs) to achieve "brain gain" by attracting specialists such as scientists, engineers, and health professionals. In contrast, less developed countries (LDCs) face the reality of "brain-drain" resulting from this migration process. While "brain loss" is used to characterize qualified migrants who immigrate from source countries to the destination country, "brain gain" emphasizes the destination country's ability to raise its global competitiveness by increasing its knowledge and technology through immigration. For a considerable period of time, brain-drain has been one of the most controversial issues for scholars, especially those researching migration. This is because there is an imbalance between its negative effects on the economic growth and development of source countries and the gains of destination countries in innovation, technology, and the labor market. While source countries lose human capital through the migration of highly skilled individuals, destination countries transform this outflow into a strategic advantage and advance in critical areas such as science, health, and technology.

The term brain-drain was first used in publications of the British Royal Society in the 1960s to explain the tendency of British scientists to immigrate to the US (Wächter, 2006, p. 54). Brain-drain gained broader usage in the context of growth and development policies in the 1970s and 1980s and was seen as an outcome of post-World War II restructuring, industrial and technological processes, and neoliberal policies (Tannock, 2007). As DCs attract highly skilled individuals to boost their scientific and technological capacity and enrich their human capital, LDCs face growing setbacks, losing vital economic and social investments and experiencing a widening developmental divide (Oteiza, 1996, p. 7). In economic terms, brain-drain is associated with the concept of "human capital," underscoring the economic value of education, skills, and talents. In an ethical and political context, the focus is on whether immigration creates injustice in favor of DCs (Kollar, 2013). Moreover, an increasing number of studies explore the effects of brain-drain through the lens of globalization (Cao, 1996; Docquier & Rapoport, 2012), post-colonialism (Rizvi, 2005; Raghuram, 2009), and exploitation (Bou-Habib, 2022; Gürak, 2024a).

According to Giannoccolo's study (2009, p. 9), which covers nearly 400 articles on the brain-drain phenomenon, in the 1950s–1960s, brain-drain was characterized by political and social causes and negative effects on welfare and social structure in the source countries; in the period up to the 1970s, international cooperation and mutual gain were presented as alternative solutions to prevent brain-drain. In the 1970s, as migration from LDCs to DCs negatively affected economic development, proposals for international coordination, such as brain-drain taxes, came to the fore. In the 1980s, the role of human capital in economic growth and technology emerged to prominence and repatriation incentives were proposed to reduce the gap between DCs and LDCs. In the 1990–2000 period, the individual motivations of immigrants (income and social factors) and the micro dimensions of migration gained more importance, and the concept of "brain gain" started to be used in the studies to emphasize the positive effects of migration.

These eras underscore the various phases that studies on brain-drain have undergone; however, the outcome of the asymmetric structure that emerged after migration has still not been sufficiently discussed, particularly in the healthcare sector. The evolution of the brain-drain phenomenon is still underway, and despite the use of more moderate language in recent discourse (such as emphasizing the potential benefits for source countries to suggest mutual gain rather than one-sided exploitation), it continues to pose a growing challenge, particularly for developing countries. Particularly in an era where imperialism extends beyond merely economic and military dimensions (Tauscher & Eskicioglu, 2025), it also maintains continuity with the phenomenon of brain-drain.

Global migration inflicts greater harm than benefit on LDC economies, as it results in the loss of a crucial segment of their highly skilled human capital, an essential yet scarce resource developed under challenging conditions and vital for economic growth and prosperity (Gürak, 2009, p. 123). Among the negative effects of brain-drain, LDCs face economic losses (tax and education costs), declining knowledge transfer, slowing long-term growth, and institutional weakening. On the other hand, source countries can benefit from the return of immigrants, remittances, and diaspora effects (e.g., lobbying, trade, investment, and technology transfer) (Brock, 2016). According to Docquier and Rapoport (2016), brain-drain can be analyzed using a simple multiplier decomposition: **Skilled migration rate = Average migration rate x Schooling Gap**. The multiplicative model for understanding the skilled migration rate is derived by multiplying the average migration rate, which indicates a country's openness to immigration, by the education gap, which indicates the probability of skilled individuals migrating. The average migration rate is the ratio of migrants to the total population. The education gap is used to explain that highly educated individuals tend to migrate in search of better opportunities. In terms of income groups, the highest migration rates are observed in middle-income countries. Individuals in these countries have sufficient incentives to migrate as well as economic and social opportunities. Therefore, the fact that large-scale and developed Western and Gulf countries (Saudi Arabia, Qatar, the UAE) are investing more and more in HC and mobility affects middle-scale and developing countries the most.

According to the World Migration Report 2024, the number of international migrants worldwide is approximately 281 million by 2020, representing 3.6% of the world population (p. 4). In the category of labor migrants, this figure was set at 169 million in 2019. Considering the report's data, the majority of migrants migrate from developing countries to larger economies (e.g., the US, Germany, Saudi Arabia). However, migration routes from low- and middle-income countries to high-income countries are on the rise. According to the World Development Report 2024 titled "The Middle Income Trap" (pp. 2–4), source countries for skilled migration are generally middle- and low-income countries (e.g., India, Türkiye, Brazil, South Africa), with most out-migration due to economic stagnation, political constraints, and low opportunities (World Bank, 2024). Destination countries are developed economies such as the US, Canada, Germany, the UK, and Singapore. Destination countries are increasingly attracting skilled labor in the health, engineering, and technology sectors through innovative policies and substantial R&D investments.

It is often the case that highly skilled individuals are highly inclined to emigrate in pursuit of better living conditions, primarily due to economic motivations (Gürak, 2024a, p. 415). On the other hand, the drivers of international mobility are not limited to economic factors; cultural and political factors also play an important role. For example, strong diasporic networks are vital as they encourage people to perceive migration as a usual phenomenon and provide a supportive environment for managing complex mobility processes (Rizvi, 2005, p. 176). Kwok and Leland (1982) argue that the root cause of brain-drain goes beyond the lack of opportunities or low wages in source countries, emphasizing instead the issue of asymmetric information in the labor market, where employers in destination countries possess greater knowledge about the productivity of foreign graduates. As a result, this knowledge has a major impact on managing skilled migration.

Brain-drain has pros and cons for source countries. As Docquier (2014) points out, brain-drain contributes to human capital accumulation in source countries by increasing investment in education and skills development; regular remittances from migrants reduce poverty and improve living standards; and diaspora communities lower international transaction costs by facilitating trade, technology transfer, and foreign investment. Moreover, the knowledge and capital acquired by returning migrants promote entrepreneurship, technology adoption, and productivity growth, while the presence of the diaspora has positive effects on democratization, institutional quality, and international visibility.

Regarding brain-drain, LDCs, particularly, have begun to pursue strategies to benefit more from their diasporas living in the transnational space through diaspora policies and public diplomacy (Hopyar et al., 2022). For example, Indian immigrants in the US contributed to the growth of information technology services in India through outsourcing during the 1990s. Members of the diaspora shared both their technical know-how and business networks with Indian entrepreneurs, enabling India's IT sector to become globally competitive (especially through their influence in Silicon Valley) and supported the local start-up ecosystem through targeted investments (Docquier & Rapoport, 2012, pp. 716–718). On the flip side of the coin, brain-drain can lead to financial losses in source countries by preventing a return on investment in education and causing labor shortages in critical sectors such as health, engineering, and technology. While a decline in HC slows economic growth and deepens poverty, distortions in the occupational structure can push individuals into low-demand fields. HC concentrated in DCs increases the gap in technological innovation and institutional development, making progress difficult for developing countries. As a result, a form of exploitation emerges, in which wealthier nations benefit disproportionately from the talents and resources of developing countries without adequately compensating for their loss.

Brain-Drain in the Healthcare Sector

It is inevitable that brain-drain affects LDCs and has both negative and positive effects on their development. Health professionals represent an essential group in the flow of highly skilled and educated individuals from LDCs to DCs. Brain-drain from LDCs to DCs is a long-standing phenomenon in the health professions. The Edinburgh Commonwealth Medical Conference in 1965 was one of the first places where the international mobility of health professionals was discussed in the last century (Martineau et al., 2004, p. 1). Following the developments discussed at the conference, in the 1970s, the World Health Organization (WHO) published a comprehensive report on the number and movement of health professionals covering 40 countries. According to this report, 90% of migrating physicians had settled in just five countries; Australia, Canada, Germany, the UK, and the US. By 1972, around 6% of physicians worldwide (140,000 people) were practicing outside their country of birth. The vast majority of these physicians had migrated to the US, the UK, and Canada, respectively (Dodani & LaPorte, 2005, p. 487). During these periods, historical colonial cultural ties were crucial in determining migration patterns, and a high proportion of health professional migrants from Commonwealth countries, mainly from India and the Caribbean, migrated to English-speaking Global North countries (Martineau et al., 2004, p. 2).

In the early 2000s, the post-colonial process became much more advanced and particularly affected African countries. Africa, as the continent with the highest concentration of health needs and problems, witnessed a migration of approximately 23,000 qualified academic professionals each year in the 2000s (Pang et al., 2002). According to data from medical schools in South Africa, between 33% and 50% of graduates immigrate to DCs. Asian countries stand out in the loss of nurses, with Filipino nurses working abroad reaching 150,000 and Zimbabwean nurses exceeding 18,000 in the same period (Pang et al., 2002). In 2006, the WHO reported that 36 out of 57 countries in Sub-Saharan Africa were experiencing severe shortages of health professionals (Kalipeni et al., 2012, p. 153). Between 2000 and 2010, the number of immigrant doctors and health workers in OECD countries increased by over 60%, and by 2014, 17.3% of physicians had been trained abroad, with the US and the UK hosting the highest numbers of foreign-trained physicians while this migration helps reduce training costs and increases reliance on existing health infrastructure (Feld, 2021). While the migration of healthcare professionals may help reduce training costs in receiving countries, it contributes to a growing reliance on the medical education systems and health infrastructures of less-resourced nations, raising important questions about sustainability, equity, and the long-term consequences for global health systems.

Brain-drain of health professionals can also be explained by push factors in source countries, active recruitment activities, and pull factors in recipient countries. According to Muula (2005), push factors driving skilled migration include limited educational opportunities, low salaries, poor prospects for career advancement, and insufficient equipment and resources in health facilities, whereas pull factors consist of higher wages, access to advanced training and specialization, and the presence of modern, well-equipped healthcare institutions in destination countries.

Young, well-educated, and healthy individuals are more likely to immigrate, especially in search of better education and economic opportunities. Inequalities in working conditions reinforce the "pull" effect between DCs and LDCs, and government policies or recruitment agencies encouraging healthcare workers to migrate further reinforce this trend (Dodani & LaPorte, 2005, pp. 487–488). Recruitment factors include aggressive advertising, active activities of recruitment agents, and supporting networks of previously migrated individuals (Muula, 2005). The weakening of healthcare systems in source countries contrasts with the advantage gained by recipient countries, which benefit from the situation to strengthen their own systems.

In addition to economic, social, and psychological factors, migrant health professionals make decisions by considering the advantages for their families. Low salaries and job conditions that reduce motivation influence the decision-making process, along with advantages such as working in better-equipped hospitals, opportunities for professional development, and the possibility of improving their families' well-being (Dodani & LaPorte, 2005, pp. 487–488). As the healthcare infrastructure weakens in source countries, the provision of healthcare services in rural areas deteriorates even further (Martineau et al., 2004). Moreover, the shortage of health professionals deepens inequitable distribution, leading to deterioration in reproductive and sexual health services and high maternal and neonatal mortality rates.

Brain-drain also negatively affects maternal, newborn, and child health; creates obstacles in the fight against HIV+/AIDS; and causes source countries to lose potential employers, academics, and role models (Serour, 2009, p. 175). Studies on brain-drain, particularly focusing on medium-sized and African countries, have gained prominence in the twenty-first century. Research indicates that the total cost of training doctors who migrate from Sub-Saharan African countries to Australia, Canada, the UK, and the US amounts to approximately USD 2 billion (Mills et al., 2011). According to a study on Kenya (Kirigia et al., 2006), the total cost of educating a medical doctor from primary school to university is USD 65,997, and each emigrating doctor costs the country approximately USD 517,931 in lost return on investment. Similarly, the total cost of educating a nurse from primary school to the College of Health Sciences is USD 43,180, and each nurse who migrates costs the country approximately

USD 338,868 in lost return on investment. Therefore, migration in the health sector has a financial dimension in addition to lagging behind in health services, the emergence of a shortage of trained specialized personnel, and adversely affecting the general public health.

Highly Skilled Migration from Türkiye

In terms of Türkiye's migration process, the labor agreements signed mostly with Western countries as of the 1960s have an important place. According to Abadan-Unat (2002, p. 38), the Turkish outward migration flow, which was first directed to Germany and then to other countries since the second half of the 1950s, went through five specific migration processes: the 1950s were characterized by migration through individual initiatives and private intermediaries; the 1960s saw an increase in state-regulated labor export based on bilateral agreements; the 1970s were marked by economic crises, the cessation of foreign worker recruitment, and family reunifications; the 1980s focused on issues such as children's education, ghetto life, association movements, rising asylum requests, and laws encouraging return migration; the 1990s witnessed the enactment of foreigner laws, the acquisition of identity by migrants, increasing xenophobia, the proliferation of ethnic businesses, the expansion of ethnic and religious associations, and demands for political rights.

In Türkiye, brain-drain became a matter of growing concern and started to be publicly discussed in the 1970s. However, in the 1980s and 1990s, the agenda fell off due to the political and economic conditions in the country, and the discussions faded (Köser-Akçapar, 2006). The post-2000s, on the other hand, has been a period in which highly skilled individuals migrated abroad (Güngör & Tansel, 2008). Before 2000, especially through the Ankara Agreement signed in 1963, an association agreement between Türkiye and the European Economic Community came into force with the goal of free movement, but the migration process remained limited due to economic changes and political concerns (Martin et al., 2001). The 1999 Helsinki Summit marked a significant turning point, as Türkiye was officially recognized as a candidate for European Union membership negotiations. Following this development, Türkiye began to accelerate the formulation of migration policies aligned with EU standards. These reforms have focused particularly on facilitating the mobility of highly skilled individuals and attracting international labor. Since then, initiatives such as Erasmus+ and the EU Blue Card scheme have contributed to an increase in skilled migration from Türkiye to the EU (Sanchez-Montijano et al., 2018).

The 2001 economic crisis played a significant role in driving the migration of qualified individuals from Türkiye in the 2000s, a trend further accelerated by the declining availability of domestic job opportunities. At the same time, rising global demand for skilled labor from DCs created attractive prospects for Turkish professionals, especially in fields such as technology and academia. According to Güngör and Tansel (2014), the integration of Turkish graduate students into foreign labor markets significantly reduces their likelihood of returning, exacerbating the country's "student non-return" problem. Moreover, economic instability and political uncertainty in Türkiye continue to reinforce the tendency of skilled individuals to remain abroad, with female migrants in particular showing lower return rates due to greater personal freedoms and lifestyle choices available overseas. In a recent field study, Hopyar (2023, pp. 96–98) examines the return experiences of skilled Turkish migrants in Germany, identifying key motivations such as discrimination, a sense of foreignness, bureaucratic challenges, weak social ties, family related reasons, and homesickness. These are primarily categorized as adaptation-related difficulties, followed by lifestyle preferences, identity issues, economic concerns, and political incentives. For skilled migrants from Türkiye, another factor influencing the decision to return is the experience of Islamophobia, social exclusion, and various forms of discrimination, which also carry a discursive dimension of hierarchical degradation imposed by the West (Bezci, 2017, p. 7). Despite their educational background, migrants may still be perceived as the "other" in multiple ways.

The Türkiye-Germany migration corridor is still one of the most prominent corridors among international migrant movements (McAuliffe & Oucho, 2024, p. 23). The historical and cultural dimension of migration between the two countries has led to the emergence of a migration corridor since the 1960s. Faist (1998) argues that migration is a result of existing economic and political structures and emphasizes the importance of addressing the regular migration flows between two or more regions or countries and the social, economic, cultural, and political connections underlying these flows. This mobility process between Türkiye and Germany continues today through skilled migration as well.

According to the statistics released by the Turkish Statistical Institute (TÜİK), the number of people migrating from Türkiye to abroad increased by 53% in 2023 compared to the previous year, reaching 714,579. Of the emigrant population, 55.2% were men while 44.8% were women. Among those who migrated from Türkiye, 291,377 were Turkish citizens, while 423,202 were foreign nationals. An analysis of the age groups of those migrating to Türkiye in 2023 shows that the highest proportion belonged to the 20–24 age group, accounting for 12.7% of the total. This was followed by the 25–29 age group at 10.8% and the 15–19 age group at 10.3%. Regarding the age distribution of those emigrating from Türkiye, the largest group was the 25–29 age category, making up 15% of the total. This was followed by the 30–34 age group at 12.9% and the 20–24 age group at 12.5% (TÜİK, 2024a, July 19).

Additionally, the brain-drain rate among higher education graduates increased from 1.6% in 2015 to 2.0% in 2023. In 2023, the brain-drain rate among female higher education graduates was 1.6%, while for male graduates, it was 2.4%. This indicates that 2 out of every 100 university graduates in Türkiye migrated abroad (TÜİK, 2024b, September 26).

As illustrated in Graph 3.1, the most preferred destination countries for graduates who completed their undergraduate programs were the US (21.4%), Germany (17.5%), the UK (11.2%), the Netherlands (6.9%), and Canada (4.9%). This trend has also begun to be observed in the university preferences of graduates from top-tier high schools in Türkiye, as they increasingly prioritize studying abroad. The fact that 146 out of 155 students out of 2024 graduates of Istanbul Erkek Lisesi (Istanbul High School), one of the highest-scoring high schools in Türkiye, chose universities in Germany and Switzerland for their university education, and only nine graduates will remain in Türkiye to continue their education (Yüksel, 2024, October 20) shows the current level of brain-drain.

As shown in Table 3.1, Germany, which is at the front rank of Türkiye's migration mobility, is leading the way with 200,000 work visas issued to recruit qualified workers. After India, Türkiye ranks second with 11,000 work visas, while Balkan countries such as Serbia (10,000), Kosovo (9000), Bosnia-Herzegovina (8000), North Macedonia (6000), and Albania (6000) have a significant share in the total for non-EU countries. Among Asian countries, Vietnam and China stood out with 8000 visas each. The high representation of small-scale countries in the Balkans shows that Germany takes geographical proximity, economic conditions, and talent pools into account.

According to Bundesärztekammer (German Medical Association) 2023 data, 63,767 foreign physicians work in health institutions in Germany as illustrated in Graph 3.2. Thus, 15% of the 428 thousand physicians

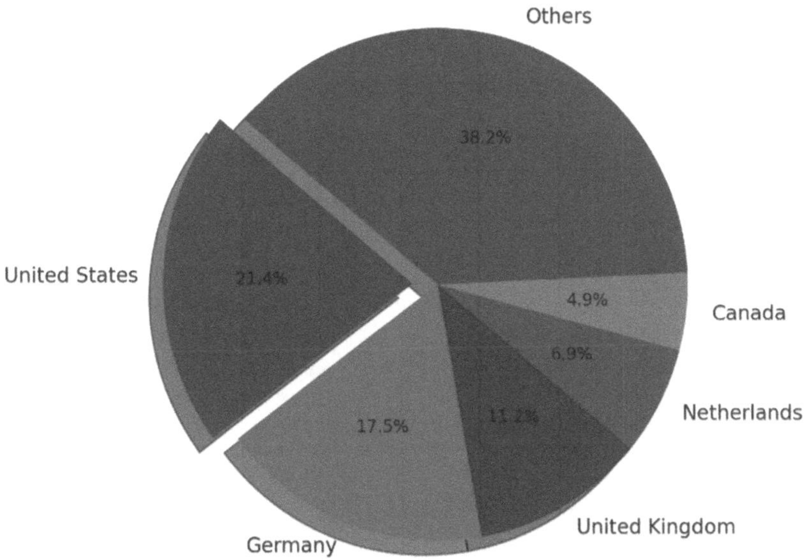

Graph 3.1 Most preferred destination countries for graduates who completed their undergraduate programs in Türkiye. (Source: *Yükseköğretim beyin göçü istatistikleri* (*Higher education brain-drain statistics*), *2021–2023*. Türkiye İstatistik Kurumu2024b, https://data.tuik.gov.tr/Bulten/Index?p=Yuksekogretim-Beyin-Gocu-Istatistikleri-2021-2023-53839#:~:text=Y%C3%BCksek%C3%B6%C4%9Fretim%20mezunlar%C4%B1n%C4%B1n%20beyin%20g%C3%B6%C3%A7%C3%BC%20oran%C4%B1,%252%2C4%20olarak%20ger%C3%A7ekle%C5%9Fti, 2025.01.13)

working in the country are foreign physicians. In 1996, only 11,039 foreign physicians were working in Germany, and the number of foreign physicians has increased significantly, especially after the 2010s. While the majority of foreign physicians come from EU countries (23,852), there are 13,557 from non-EU European countries, with Asia (17,160) and Africa (5697) standing out as important source continents (Bundesärztekammer, 2023, p. 38).

The US holds a significant position as another key destination country for skilled migration from Türkiye. Between 1956 and 1970, 907 engineers and 594 physicians migrated to the US from Türkiye (Oğuzkan, 1976, p. 78).

Table 3.1 Number of work visas issued by Germany by country in 2024

Country	*Number of work visas*
India	20,000
Türkiye	11,000
Serbia	10,000
Kosovo	9000
Vietnam	8000
China	8000
Bosnia and Herzegovina	8000
North Macedonia	6000
Albania	6000
Other countries	114,000
Total	**200,000**

Source: Gemeinsame Pressemitteilung des AA, BMAS und BMI: Ein Jahr neues Fachkräfteeinwanderungsgesetz: Zahlen ausländischer Fachkräfte, Studierender und Auszubildender steigen deutlich. *Auswärtiges Amt(2024)*. https://www.auswaertiges-amt.de/de/newsroom/2684922-2684922, 2025.01.05

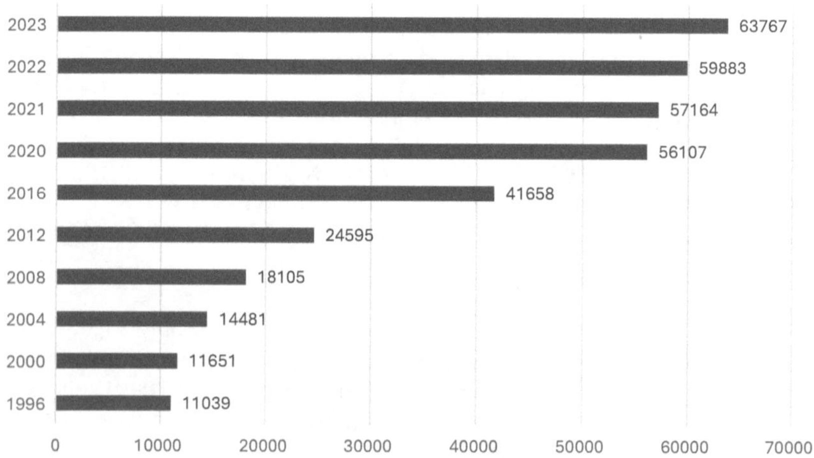

Graph 3.2 Number of foreign physicians working in Germany by year. (Source: Ärztestatistik zum 31. Dezember 2023. Bundesärztekammer. https://www.bundesaerztekammer.de/fileadmin/user_upload/BAEK/Ueber_uns/Statistik/AErztestatistik_2023_18.04.2024.pdf, 2025.01.08)

In 1970, 82 Turkish scientists and engineers who migrated to the US accounted for only 0.6% of the 13,337 global scientist and engineer migrants, while 44 Turkish medical doctors constituted 1.4% of the total 3155 medical migrant professionals in the same year (Oğuzkan, 1976). However, this loss was significant for Türkiye. According to a United Nations report, the migration of highly skilled professionals from Türkiye to the US, France, and Canada between 1962 and 1966 resulted in a loss equivalent to 7% of the country's trained engineers, 16% of its natural scientists, and 15% of its medical doctors (Oğuzkan, 1976, p. 80). As of 2020, among the 55,918 individuals who graduated from an undergraduate program in Türkiye between 2009 and 2013 and subsequently migrated abroad, the most preferred destination countries were the US (22.4%), Germany (14.3%), and the UK (11.6%) (Metin, 2023, p. 395). Today, Türkiye ranks 20th in the list of international student source countries. In the 2023/24 academic year, the number of international students traveling from Türkiye to the US reached 9148, an increase of 5.7% compared to the previous year. Although there was a decline in 2020/21 due to the global pandemic, student mobility has been on the rise again in the following years. Among Turkish students, 33.6% prefer US universities for undergraduate education and 45.1% for graduate education, with 82.9% preferring universities with PhD education opportunities. In 2024, there was a 6.3% increase in student visas, with states such as New York, California, and Massachusetts being the preferred states (Opendoors, n.d.).

Skilled migrants cannot always work in jobs requiring qualifications and expertise in their host countries. This concept, called "brain waste," generally refers to individuals' knowledge, expertise, skills, talents, and potentials not adequately utilized or effectively employed in their careers (Batalova et al., 2016). According to a 2008 study by Mattoo, Neagu, and Özden on the occupational placement of highly educated immigrants in the US labor market, a college graduate from India has a 69% probability of being placed in a skilled job, compared to 24% for an immigrant from Mexico. While the researchers attribute the brain waste to the fact that the professional success of migrants is directly related to the quality of education, English language training, and investments in human capital in their countries of origin, factors such as lack of recognition of professional qualifications, differences between education systems and political instability are among the leading causes of brain waste. Skilled individuals who leave Türkiye to live abroad may choose unskilled jobs instead of their professions as migration options. As a result, especially on social media, they show their experiences, such as "Türkiye lost an engineer/medical doctor, but country X (destination countries) gained a minimum wage earner." The brain waste experienced becomes viral and normalized with derivatives of this expression. Moreover, this situation leads to a loss of skilled labor from Türkiye and further contributes to a long-term waste of potential, as many migrants face career stagnation or decline in their destination countries.

Migration of Health Professionals from Türkiye

Brain-drain in Türkiye has reached a remarkable level in the last decade, with thousands of physicians and nurses leaving for high-income countries. For LDCs, the priority is **skilled mental labor** that can effectively apply existing technologies, rather than creative mental labor that invents new technologies (Gürak, 2024b, pp. 88–90); in this context, physicians and nurses who already have experience in the field of health are among the main actors that make existing technology and structure sustainable. Physicians who will work abroad are asked to provide a record of whether they have any negative records regarding their professional activities. As in all countries, professional audits of physicians in Türkiye are carried out by professional organizations. For this reason, the relevant institutions must request the registration documents for physicians from the Turkish Medical Association (Türk Tabipleri Birliği), the professional organization of physicians. Therefore, the good standing certificate provided by the Turkish Medical Association constitutes an important source of reference for reaching the number of physicians migrating from Türkiye to abroad.

According to data released by the Turkish Medical Association, 3025 physicians applied for a certificate of good standing to work abroad in the first 11 months of 2023 (Turkish Medical Association, 2023). As shown in Graph 3.3, the total number over the past ten years has reached 5035. Considering that this number was 90 only ten years ago, it is seen that there has been a big break, especially after 2016–2017, and the number of health workers who want to go abroad has increased dramatically.

According to OECD data for 2021, there are 2.2 medical doctors per thousand people in Türkiye. The OECD average is 3.7 doctors per thousand people. Türkiye ranks last among OECD members in the number of doctors per capita (OECD, 2023, p. 177). Türkiye is also second to last in the number of nurses per capita. As of 2021, the number of nurses in Türkiye is below three per thousand people. Considering that the OECD

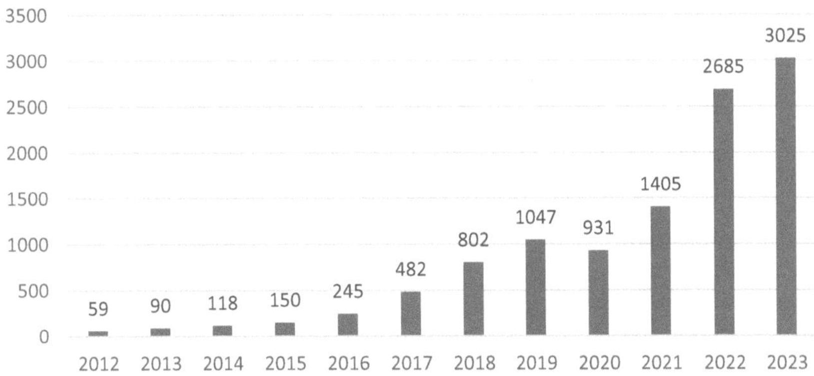

Graph 3.3 Number of physicians receiving "Good Standing Certificates". (Source: Turkish Medical Association—Türk Tabipleri Birliği [@ttborgtr]. (2023, December 29). TTB'ye "İyi Hal Belgesi" başvuru sayısı; Aralık ayında 240, 2023 yılında 3025 oldu. [Tweet]. Twitter. https://x.com/ttborgtr/status/1740746140457279822, 2025.01.05)

average is 9.2 nurses per thousand people, the low number of nurses in Türkiye clearly shows the shortage of nurses in the health system. Thus, Türkiye is at similar levels with countries such as Colombia and Mexico in terms of the number of nurses per capita. Moreover, while there has been a general increase in the number of nurses in OECD countries in the last decade, the increase in Türkiye has been limited compared to other countries (OECD, 2023). Therefore, the brain-drain phenomenon in health is one of the areas that need to be examined for Türkiye due to both the difficulty of educating health professionals and its impact on the health sector, which is one of the most significant development indicators of a country.

Training and recruiting physicians and nurses into the workforce are vital for any country. The first empirical study on health brain-drain in Türkiye was a joint study of medical doctors conducted in 1968 by the Ankara Institute of Public Health and the Johns Hopkins School of Public Health. The main reasons for Turkish medical doctors to migrate abroad included insufficient income, professional promotion difficulties, and health system deficiencies (Elveren, 2018, p. 39). According to the UN, 375 Turkish scientists emigrated between 1962 and 1967; 51.1% were medical doctors, 40% were engineers, 5.5% were scientists, and 3% were social scientists (Erkal, 1980, cited in Elveren, 2018, p. 39).

In a study conducted by Kurnaz Ay et al. (2024) to examine the migration motivations and experiences of 506 health professionals who migrated from Türkiye between April and June 2022, it was reported that the leading reasons for migration motivations were the political environment in the country, lack of freedom of expression, violence in the health sector, and deteriorating working conditions. While participants faced trauma, uncertainty, and economic difficulties during the migration process, the most significant problems after migration were language barriers and slow bureaucratic processes. Nevertheless, factors such as the democratic structure of society abroad, security, and freedom of expression are said to have made participants' lives more peaceful. According to the study, most participants stated that their primary objective is to complete the professional equivalence process by enhancing their language proficiency and integrating into the society of their host country.

Kilic et al. (2019) examined the migration tendencies of psychiatry residents in Türkiye, investigating the rate of those who plan to migrate and the reasons affecting this decision. The study included 107 psychiatry residents in Türkiye, and it was concluded that 75% of them were considering living abroad, but only 4.7% wanted to settle for the long term. Among the reasons for migration, academic inadequacies, challenging working conditions, and financial difficulties stand out, while language barriers, bureaucracy, and cultural ties are noted as factors that complicate migration. In addition, participants emphasized that improving education and working conditions could reduce the tendency to migrate.

Ulupinar et al. (2024) used a mixed-method research design in their research on nurse's attitudes toward brain-drain in Türkiye and collected quantitative data from 1018 participants and qualitative data from 26 volunteers. The findings revealed that 84.3% of the participants wanted to work abroad, 95% saw a risk of brain-drain in nursing and cited economic factors as the main reason. It was also found that the brain-drain tendency decreased with age and experience, but nurses and nursing students tend to migrate more than academicians.

Although factors such as language barriers, bureaucracy, and cultural ties make migration difficult, they do not fundamentally eliminate the migration trend. In other words, it is seen that the migration decision has matured structurally but has been delayed only due to some technical and social obstacles, and there is a danger that DCs may increase the migration rates even further with new legal regulations regarding the migration of healthcare professionals. Therefore, although the salary increase for healthcare professionals initially slows down the brain-drain for Türkiye, there is the potential to stop migration only with multidimensional improvements such as institutional support, career development, academic advancement opportunities, and humanitarianization of working environments.

Migration mobility between Türkiye and Germany is also reflected in healthcare services. Tezcan's study (2018) examines the circular migration behavior of elderly Turkish migrants in Germany and the effects of this migration on health services, perceived health status, and elderly care. The research reveals that senior migrants often return to Germany due to Germany's advanced healthcare system, while Türkiye offers a health-enhancing lifestyle by offering religious, psychological, and physical comfort. Based on 40 in-depth interviews, the study shows that elderly care is shaped by intra-family conflict and exchange relations, weakening traditional family solidarity. Participants stated that the time they spent in Türkiye positively impacted their health and that their dependence on the health system in Germany made their migration permanent. While this "between-countries" way of living creates unique challenges in both host and origin countries, it also offers a two-way strategy to meet the health and care needs of older migrants.

Türkiye has become an important destination for health tourism in recent years. Areas such as plastic surgery, eye treatments, oncology, and orthopedics are among Türkiye's prominent health services (Kılıçarslan, 2019). According to a study by Omay and Cengiz (2013), Türkiye has increased the number of international patients from 74,093 in 2008 to 270,000 in 2012 and has become a global center of attraction in the field of health tourism with its JCI-accredited hospitals and affordable price advantages (e.g., heart bypass surgery costs USD 130,000 in the US and USD 11,000–USD 15,000 in Türkiye), and this sector has added significant growth potential to Türkiye's USD 26 billion tourism revenue. On the other hand, in 2012, Türkiye generated an average revenue of USD 728 per tourist, while Germany, despite hosting fewer tourists (17% fewer), generated about 47% more revenue than Türkiye. In 2018, the number of health tourists visiting Türkiye, which continues to rise in the health tourism sector, increased to 551,748 (Ceti & Unluonen, 2020). In 2018, Türkiye's total tourism revenues amounted to USD 29.5 billion, of which USD 863 million was generated from health tourism (Ceti & Unluonen, 2020, p. 105).

Cost of Brain-Drain in Health for Türkiye

The brain-drain results in both the loss of the financial investment made for individuals' development and education in their home country and the social and cultural losses left behind as qualified individuals emigrate. This situation creates a substantial challenge for developing countries. Skilled professionals, such as doctors, engineers, and academics, are essential for addressing domestic issues and supporting innovation. When they emigrate, the source country loses the investment made in their education and training and the critical contributions they could make to society. This loss is compounded by the permanence of their departure, which means these professionals are less likely to return and contribute to their home countries' growth. Meanwhile, DCs benefit economically by filling high-demand roles without bearing the initial educational costs. These dynamics underscore a global inequality where talent flows from the places most in need to those already resource-rich, perpetuating developmental disparities between countries.

In the study conducted by Şen Olgay and Yurt in 2023 to determine the reasons for migration and life satisfaction of health professionals migrating from Türkiye to the UK, and in which 128 health professionals participated, the data were collected using the Sociodemographic Data Collection Form and Life Satisfaction Scale, the average age of the participants was 41.20±10.56; 28.1% of the participants were nurses, and it was finally determined that 89.8% experienced professional satisfaction in the UK and 95.3% were satisfied with living in the UK. Among the reasons for migration (see Graph 3.4), political reasons account for 64.8%, concerns about the future for 55.5%, and economic reasons for 53.1% stand out as the most prominent factors (Şen Olgay & Yurt, 2023, p. 99).

According to a 2021 study involving 161 resident physicians employed at university and state hospitals in Ankara, the capital of Türkiye, researchers explored the perspectives of these healthcare professionals on brain-drain and job satisfaction (Uğur, 2022). The study used a comprehensive questionnaire, including the Minnesota Job Satisfaction Scale, to measure job satisfaction levels and examine physicians' attitudes toward potential emigration. The findings indicated that over half of the participants were interested in pursuing medical specialty programs abroad, with 51.6% (83 out of 161) expressing a desire for further specialization internationally. Additionally, 55.3% (89 out of 161) reported a general intention to seek employment abroad. The countries most frequently cited for these

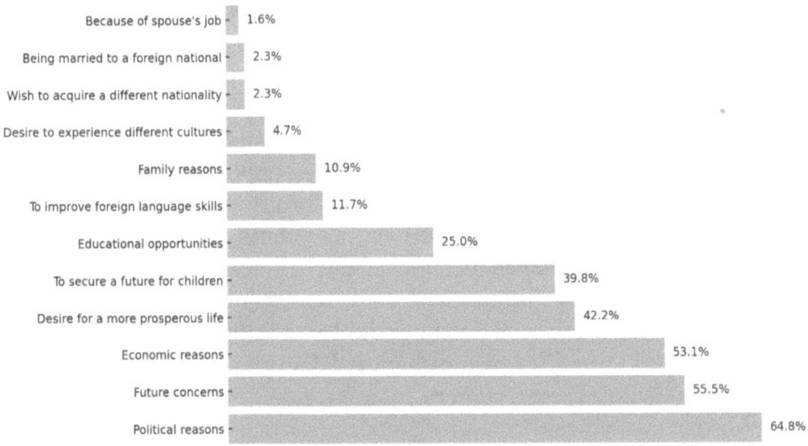

Graph 3.4 Reasons for healthcare professionals' migration to the UK. (Source: Şen Olgay, S., & Yurt, S. (2023). Türkiye'den İngiltere'ye göç eden sağlık çalışanlarının göç nedenleri ve yaşam doyumlarının belirlenmesi. *Sağlık ve Hemşirelik Yönetimi Dergisi, 10*(1), 99–107, p. 103)

educational and professional aspirations were Germany, the US, England, and Canada. Another study conducted on physicians receiving education at GATA in 2014 found that the estimated cost per student, including adjustments for inflation and program expenses, reached approximately 268,840 TL (equivalent to USD 180,000 at the exchange rate for that year) for the entire six-year program by the 2009–2010 academic year (Abuhanoğlu et al., 2014).

A cross-sectional study conducted in 2022 included 9881 final-year medical students from 39 different medical schools in Türkiye (Eser et al., 2024). The study assessed participants' migration intentions, as well as the push and pull factors related to working conditions, social environment, lifestyle, educational adequacies, and socio-economic variables that might influence their decision to migrate abroad. Eser et al.'s study (2024, p. 2) found that 70.7% of medical students intended to emigrate. Approximately 60% of students expressed a desire to remain abroad permanently, and 61.5% had undertaken steps toward migration, such as learning a foreign language (54.5%) or taking relevant exams (18.9%). According to the study, the primary push factor associated with emigration intent was "working conditions in the country," while "social environment/lifestyle abroad" emerged as the main pull factor. Additionally, the perceived quality issues in medical schools significantly influenced students' decisions.

When the migration tendencies of the health sector in Türkiye are analyzed in general, driving factors such as difficult working conditions, low salaries, limited career opportunities, economic instability, and future concerns lead health professionals to seek better opportunities in DCs. In addition, infrastructural inadequacies of the healthcare system and workplace conditions are other important factors behind this decision. On the other hand, pull factors such as high salaries, attractive career opportunities and modern health facilities in DCs increase the tendency of qualified individuals in the health sector to migrate. In addition to these factors, the support networks provided by transnational diaspora communities and the assistance of employment centers in migration processes facilitate the decision-making of healthcare professionals, particularly in today's world, where communication and transportation technologies have advanced, and globalization has intensified. Therefore, it is observed that Tertiary Determinants, namely personal networks and social encouragement, as highlighted by Portes (1976), have become significantly more influential in decision-making within the context of brain-drain.

Infrastructures that are not directly visible apart from educational expenses but are necessary for education and workspace also impose expenses. Considering the extra costs, when the document titled "Minimum conditions for starting and continuing education in medical programs" announced by the Council of Higher Education (Yükseköğretim Kurulu-YÖK) is reviewed, the cost of medical education to the state in Türkiye includes many elements ranging from physical infrastructure requirements such as classrooms, laboratories, libraries to the bed capacity, and medical device needs of university hospitals. Operating a university hospital with a 200-bed capacity for 60 students, laboratory equipment such as anatomy, physiology, histology, and microbiology, medical skills training laboratories, and patient simulation rooms represent significant cost items. In addition, for every 60 students, there is a need for one faculty member in fields such as anatomy, physiology, pathology, pharmacology (this number increases for quotas between 60 and 120 students) and at least two to five faculty members in surgical branches. Hospital infrastructure and personnel support required for clinical practices, which are part of medical education, are among the other factors that increase costs (YÖK, n.d.).

According to the laws of migration expressed by Ravenstein (1885), migration does not tolerate a void, and the places emptied as a result of migration are subsequently filled with new migrations. Wallerstein (2020) divides the world, where capitalism prevails, into the periphery, semi-periphery, and core. The core-periphery approach, which is frequently used to explain migration processes, illustrates the flow of migration from the periphery to the core, with brain-drain serving as a significant parameter. In this system, semi-peripheral countries compete primarily with one another and strive to climb the hierarchy ladder through mutual struggles (Wallerstein, 2020). While Türkiye has been migrating health professionals to DCs, i.e., there has been mobility toward the center, foreign health professionals from peripheral countries have also migrated to Türkiye and started to work in the health sector with an increase after the 2010s. In this respect, Türkiye is in a semi-peripheral position, with 309 foreign doctors working in Türkiye in 2012, and this number reached 4242 in 2020 as we can see in Table 3.2. (Erdem, 2022, July 4). Undoubtedly, the forced migration of millions of refugees to Türkiye following the Syrian civil war that started in 2011 and Türkiye's open door policy plays an important role in the formation of this picture.

The training of medical doctors requires high public expenditures for DCs and results in health migration, with investments in developing countries benefiting developed countries. For example, in LDCs such as India

Table 3.2 Number of foreign physicians in Türkiye by year

Year	*Number of foreign physicians*
2012	309
2013	555
2014	856
2015	1056
2016	1346
2017	1574
2018	4144
2019	4603
2020	4242

Source: Erdem, A. K. (2022, July 4). 8 yılda 18 bin 685 yabancı sağlık çalışanı Türkiye'de çalışmaya başladı: Yabancılar, yurt dışına giden Türk sağlık çalışanlarının yerini doldurabilir mi? *Independent Türkçe*. https://www.indyturk.com/node/528146/sa%C4%9Flik/8-y%C4%B1lda-18-bin-685-yabanc%C4%B1-sa%C4%9Fl%C4%B1k-%C3%A7al%C4%B1%C5%9Fan%C4%B1-t%C3%BCrkiyede-%C3%A7al%C4%B1%C5%9Fmaya-ba%C5%9Flad%C4%B1-yabanc%C4%B1lar, 2025.01.20

and Pakistan, the migration of each physician trained with public funds results in a cost loss of between USD 50,000 and USD 150,000 (Adovor et al., 2021). Especially in low-income countries, physician migration increases the shortcomings in health services, leading to an increased burden of disease and greater economic losses. According to the WHO, developing countries will face a shortage of 18 million health professionals by 2030. While the economic contribution of migrating medical doctors creates serious losses for the countries to which they migrate, the economic value of a migrating doctor in regions such as Sub-Saharan Africa is estimated to be between USD 0.5 and 1 million (Adovor et al., 2021). On the other hand, developed countries such as the US, the UK, and Canada have made significant economic gains from immigrant physicians. For instance, a migrant physician in the UK contributes around 250,000 GBP per year, and 34.5% of physicians working in the UK receive their medical education in other countries (Brennan et al., 2023). According to the World Bank, this brain-drain causes losses of billions of dollars on a global scale, with Sub-Saharan Africa's annual loss estimated at USD 2 billion and India's annual loss due to doctors migrating to the US estimated at USD 1–2 billion (Adovor et al., 2021).

On the other hand, a significant majority of Turkish physicians who migrate abroad prefer Germany in the first place (Elmacıoğlu, 2021, November 21). The intensive migration flow that started with Türkiye's labor agreement with Germany dating back to the 1960s allowed the Turkish diaspora to develop mostly in Germany (Abadan-Unat, 2002). The migration flow, which developed with unskilled labor migration in the 1960s and 1970s, continued with family reunification and illegal migration, despite Germany's termination of the labor agreement in 1973. Today, this process has transformed into skilled migration and, with the continuing shortage of skilled labor in many sectors in Germany, to fill the shortage of employees in the health system. In 1993, the number of doctors of foreign origin in Germany was around 10 thousand, while this number almost tripled to 30 thousand in 2013, and then in 2023, according to the statistics of the German Federal Chamber of Doctors, 63,763 doctors without German passports were working in Germany as of December 31, 2023. The number of physicians from Türkiye practicing medicine within the German health system was announced as 2628 (Ärzteblatt, 2024, March 4).

Global Implications of Brain-Drain in the Health Sector

According to a document prepared by the German Bundestag-Research and Documentation Services (Wissenschaftliche Dienste des Deutschen Bundestages), which explains the cost and resource allocation of medical education in Germany and the economic impact of German medical students studying in other European Union countries, medical education is particularly costly in Germany's health and medical sciences programs. The most recent available data on medical costs are from 2017, and the ongoing expenditure for a medical student in Germany, excluding teaching exams, is approximately €170,500 (Deutscher Bundestag Wissenschaftliche Dienste, 2020, p. 12). According to the Federal Statistical Office, German public universities spent an average of €10,790 per student in Germany in 2013, while the average cost of a medical student to a university was €31,690 per year (Der Spiegel, 2016, February 25). Therefore, Germany, which offers more than 60,000 physicians the opportunity to work, has reduced costs by billions of euros in this respect. On the other hand, while the education cost of a medical student in the Netherlands, one of the primary destinations of migration from Türkiye and a country with a significant Turkish diaspora, is calculated by the state to be an average of €193,000, the annual education cost of a medical student in Austria has been reported to be approximately €56,823 (Deutscher Bundestag Wissenschaftliche Dienste, 2020, p. 9).

Different educational practices and university systems in different countries mean that education costs are either borne by the students themselves, covered by scholarships, or subsidized by the government. For example, in the US, medical students graduate with an average debt of USD 180,000, whereas in the UK, a largely state-supported system operates, with full tuition fees and living expenses covered by the National Health Service (NHS), especially in the last two years of education (Keane et al., 2020). Considering that in 2018, the average cost of medical and nursing education in the UK was estimated at USD 114,000 per medical doctor and USD 32,000 per nurse, gaining specialists without spending all these costs enables developed countries to gain financially in terms of health and education, as well as providing more health services to their people (Kamarulzaman et al., 2022).

According to Mills et al., 2011 study on medical school costs and total education costs in nine African countries, the highest cost of medical education is South Africa, where resources allocated for education are higher due to a more developed economic infrastructure, while the country with the lowest cost is Uganda, and the average cost in all these countries is calculated as USD 34,646 as shown in Table 3.3. These figures represent the varying economic conditions across Africa. At the same time, the countries that fully cover each individual's education expenses experience both the same financial burden and the loss of skilled professionals. Meanwhile, the destination countries benefit from acquiring experts without bearing the cost of their education, creating a highly unbalanced system.

As observed, alongside the number of physicians who have already emigrated, there are indications that this trend will continue to rise. Therefore, beyond financial costs, it is essential to calculate the socio-cultural costs of this migration. Additionally, there is a need to examine the healthcare migration policies of destination countries and to increase both the quantity and quality of academic studies that provide insights into healthcare professionals' migration from the perspective of Türkiye. However, as Gürak (2024b, pp. 98–99) argues, this structural problem cannot be addressed solely through the efforts of source countries such as Türkiye; DCs also have a critical role in mitigating brain-drain. For instance, they can support the establishment of vocational schools and technology faculties in less developed countries, sending qualified professionals to teach in these institutions. Additionally, they can promote short- or medium-term assignments for skilled experts to contribute to knowledge transfer in these contexts.

Table 3.3 Medical education costs in African countries

Country	*Medical school cost (USD)*	*Total education cost (USD)*
Ethiopia	28.620	29.898
Kenya	32.225	36.453
Malawi	32.952	34.286
Nigeria	25.188	36.410
South Africa	40.383	58.698
Tanzania	23.511	27.256
Uganda	18.870	21.040
Zambia	26.529	27.749
Zimbabwe	37.500	38.620
Average	28.542	34.646

Source: Mills et al. (2011). The financial cost of doctors emigrating from sub-Saharan Africa: human capital analysis. *BMJ*, *343*, p. 10

Reverse Brain-Drain

Reverse brain-drain refers to the phenomenon in which highly skilled individuals who have either pursued education abroad and subsequently started working overseas or migrated to developed countries for employment after completing their domestic education return to their home countries to apply the knowledge and experience they have gained. This process contributes to their countries' economic, scientific, and technological development (Wadhwa, 2009). Through reverse brain-drain, **LDCs** benefit from the expertise of individuals who have further enhanced their skills abroad while also reclaiming those who initially migrated after receiving domestic education. Particularly in countries such as India and China, increasing economic opportunities and government initiatives actively encourage migrants to return to their home countries.

China's talent-attraction policies were enacted to deal with China's brain-drain problem, which became increasingly prominent in the late twentieth century, and the relatively low return rate of Chinese students, scientists, and academics in the 1990s caused concern among government officials (Marini & Yang, 2021). According to Zweig (2006), since the 2000s, China has implemented comprehensive incentive policies at both national and local levels to increase the return rate of individuals who studied abroad. The central government has offered research funding, professional titles, and housing, while local governments have provided tax exemptions, housing subsidies, and educational opportunities for family members. Universities and research institutions have also launched programs such as the "Cheung Kong Scholars Program" and the "Hundred Talents Program" to attract highly qualified returnees. Although many of those who returned possessed greater knowledge and skills than local experts, the most competent individuals often chose to remain abroad. Moreover, the preferential treatment given to returnees has at times generated dissatisfaction among local professionals.

Under the wave of reverse migration, Chinese scholars and academics returning from abroad have gradually changed the labor force structure of Chinese academia (Lu & Zhang, 2015). This positive shift plays a key role in enabling countries to recover their resource investments and to benefit from the reintegration of transnational experiences into the national context. According to Hussain (2015), governments should offer incentives to compensate returnees for their potential income losses abroad, facilitate their full-time employment, and enhance the efficiency of these processes through microeconomic analysis. When properly managed, return migration can thus generate significant benefits for developing countries, particularly in terms of economic growth and the accumulation of human capital.

In recent years, Türkiye has started implementing policies to reverse the brain-drain process. The tendency of Turkish scientists in the diaspora to return is low. However, the tendency for intellectual contribution is high, so it is necessary to strengthen the financial structures of universities and research institutions and develop joint projects with the diaspora to encourage their return (Durmaz, 2022). The Scientific and Technological Research Council of Türkiye (TÜBİTAK) started "coordinating the EU 7th Framework Program" in 2007, which encourages reverse brain-drain of researchers for Türkiye and has organized "Introducing European and National Funding Opportunities" for scientists returning to Türkiye and "Destination Türkiye Workshops" for reverse brain-drain since 2010 (TÜBİTAK, 2015, May 14). In 2013, 44 scientists returned to Türkiye under the "Return to Türkiye Research Scholarship Program" (TÜBİTAK, 2013, October 21). Workshops were organized in a total of 12 locations in the US and Europe, reaching approximately 1500 qualified Turkish scientists in 2 continents, and 597 researchers applied for repatriation, 360 of whom were supported (TÜBİTAK, 2015, May 14). In 2018, "2232-A International Leading Researchers Program," "2232-B International Young Researchers Program," "2247-A National Leading Researchers Program," and "2247-D National Young Researchers Program," which are carried out by TÜBİTAK's Directorate of Support Programs for Scientists (Bilim Insanları Destek Programları Başkanlığı-BİDEB), were activated, and 152 Turkish citizens participated in the first call of the programs. It was reported that 243 researchers, 91 of whom were foreign nationals, applied; 173 of these applications were from the top 100 universities in the world; 31 of them were from global companies with the highest R&D expenditures in the world; and 28 of them were from the top 250 most successful public institutions and institutes in the world. As a result of the applications, 127 researchers from 21 different countries returned to Türkiye, 7 of them in the field of health sciences (TÜBİTAK, 2021, March 17).

In the healthcare sector, the "White Reform" initiative, launched in 2022, aimed to improve the rights and benefits of healthcare professionals and enhance efficiency within the healthcare system. This program has yielded significant outcomes in reducing physician migration and encouraging their return. The second phase of the program was announced in 2023, and with policies such as a more effective fight against violence in health, increasing on-call pay, and reflecting fixed payments to retirement, efforts were made both to prevent health migration and to encourage the return of outgoing doctors (Republic of Türkiye Ministry of Health, 2023a, December 22). Considering that Turkish doctors may also be migrating from Türkiye to protect their professional identity, reputation, and self-respect (Önal & Akay, 2024), regulations on personal rights and preventing violence in health facilities may increase the rate of return. According to the statements of Koca, the Minister of Health at the time, resignations from the public sector decreased by 40% after the White Reform, while the number of physicians returning to public service reached 8000 (Republic of Türkiye Ministry of Health, 2023b, September 06). It was also announced that the number of physicians who went abroad in 2022 was 450 and 55 physicians returned, while 28 of the 395 physicians who went abroad in 2023 returned (Republic of Türkiye Ministry of Health, 2023c, August 01).

Conclusion

While DCs increase their competitiveness in areas such as science, technology, and the health sector by attracting skilled and qualified individuals, LDCs face negative effects such as economic losses and long-term growth problems. Countries experiencing migration face significant challenges due to the loss of human capital and increasing inequalities. LDCs face two strategic options in achieving their development goals: either invest in developing their own technologies or transfer existing and proven technologies from DCs (Gürak, 2003, p. 6). Diaspora networks and reverse brain-drain play a significant role for LDCs in facilitating technology transfer. Diaspora communities dispersed to other countries as a result of migration provide important opportunities for source countries through their economic contributions, knowledge transfer, and impact on democratization. Therefore, the brain-drain phenomenon constitutes an asymmetrical structure that creates global inequalities with its economic, social, and political dimensions. At the same time, when it is managed effectively, it can benefit source countries through diasporic networks.

The brain-drain of health professionals is increasing significantly with the rise of globalization due to higher salaries and better working conditions in DCs. Health migration weakens the health infrastructure in source countries and leads to disruption of health services, especially in rural areas, deterioration in maternal and child health, and economic losses. In regions such as the Caribbean, South Asia, and Sub-Saharan Africa, significant financial investments in training migrant health workers have been lost. This causes serious financial, social, cultural, and medical problems in source countries while providing strategic advantages for recipient countries, especially regarding financial resources.

The increase in brain-drain in Türkiye is particularly noteworthy for those employed in the health sector. Türkiye's migration process has gained momentum since the 1960s with labor agreements with Western countries and has been shaped by changing dynamics in different periods. After the 2000s, the emigration of highly qualified individuals abroad has increased, and economic and political conditions in Türkiye have triggered this process. Today, the rate of brain-drain among higher education graduates is on the rise, with countries such as the US, Germany, and the UK being the most preferred destinations. The Türkiye-Germany migration corridor still retains its historical significance. Migration, especially in the education and health sectors, causes significant losses for Türkiye as a source country. In the last decade, Türkiye has experienced a significant increase in brain-drain, especially among health professionals. The number of physicians applying for a certificate of good conduct to work abroad increased from 90 in 2013 to over 3000 in 2023, revealing dissatisfaction with working conditions in the country. Studies show that working conditions, limited professional opportunities, and social and lifestyle advantages abroad are the main reasons for migration. Medical students and physicians often prefer countries that offer better professional environments and career opportunities, such as Germany, the US, and the UK. The financial burden of medical education on Türkiye is considerable, with education costs per student reaching high levels, further deepening the economic impact of migration. In response to this trend, Türkiye has initiated several programs to reverse the brain-drain and encourage the return of qualified professionals. In Türkiye, initiatives by TÜBITAK and the Ministry of Health have yielded partial positive results, such as fewer resignations and the return of some professionals, but Türkiye has also turned to the concept of replacing lost specialists with foreign health professionals.

References

Abadan-Unat, N. (2002). *Bitmeyen göç: Konuk işçilikten ulus-ötesi yurttaşlığa*. İstanbul Bilgi Üniversitesi Yayınları.

Abuhanoğlu, H., Ayanoğlu, Y., Cankul, İ. H., & Teke, A. (2014). Tıp eğitimi maliyeti ve eğitim sürecinde ortaya çıkan kayıpların maliyetlere etkisi. *Gülhane Tıp Dergisi, 56*(3), 147–153. https://doi.org/10.5455/gulhane.38137

Adovor, E., Czaika, M., Docquier, F., & Moullan, Y. (2021). Medical brain-drain: How many, where and why? *Journal of Health Economics, 76*, 102409. https://doi.org/10.1016/j.jhealeco.2020.102409

Ärzteblatt. (2024, March 4). Rekordzahl bei Ärzten ohne deutschen Pass. *Ärzteblatt.de*. Retrieved January 22, 2025, from https://www.aerzteblatt.de/nachrichten/149716/Rekordzahl-bei-Aerzten-ohne-deutschen-Pass

Auswärtiges Amt. (2024, November 17). Gemeinsame Pressemitteilung des AA, BMAS und BMI: Ein Jahr neues Fachkräfteeinwanderungsgesetz: Zahlen ausländischer Fachkräfte, Studierender und Auszubildender steigen deutlich. *Auswärtiges Amt*. Retrieved January 5, 2025, from https://www.auswaertiges-amt.de/de/newsroom/2684922-2684922

Batalova, J., Fix, M., & Bachmeier, J. D. (2016). *Untapped talent: The costs of brain waste among highly skilled immigrants in the United States*. World Education Services.

Bezci, B. (2017). Avrupa'da göç politikaları, İslamofobi ve aşırı sağın yükselişi. In B. Bezci, S. Tauscher, & F. Topal (Eds.), *Avrupa'da Göç ve İslamofobi* (pp. 1–18). Karınca Yayınevi.

Bou-Habib, P. (2022). The brain-drain as exploitation. *Politics, Philosophy & Economics, 21*(3), 249–268. https://doi.org/10.1177/1470594X211027259

Brennan, N., Langdon, N., Bryce, M., Burns, L., Humphries, N., Knapton, A., & Gale, T. (2023). Drivers and barriers of international migration of doctors to and from the United Kingdom: A scoping review. *Human Resources for Health, 21*(11), 1–22. https://doi.org/10.1186/s12960-022-00789-y

Brock, G. (2016). Debating brain-drain: An overview. *Moral Philosophy and Politics, 3*(1), 7–20. https://doi.org/10.1515/mopp-2015-0020

Bundesärztekammer. (2023). Ärztestatistik zum 31. Dezember 2023. Bundesärztekammer. Retrieved January 8, 2025, from https://www.bundesaerztekammer.de/fileadmin/user_upload/BAEK/Ueber_uns/Statistik/AErztestatistik_2023_18.04.2024.pdf

Cao, X. (1996). Debating 'brain-drain' in the context of globalisation. *Compare, 26*(3), 269–285. https://doi.org/10.1080/0305792960260303

Ceti, B., & Unluonen, K. (2020). Economic evaluation of health tourism in Turkey. *Journal of Tourismology, 6*(1), 99–109. https://doi.org/10.26650/jot.2020.6.1.0015

Der Spiegel. (2016, February 25). *Statistik: So viel kosten Studenten ihre Unis pro Jahr*. Der Spiegel. Retrieved February 10, 2025, from https://www.spiegel.de/lebenundlernen/uni/statistik-so-viel-kosten-studenten-ihre-unis-pro-jahr-a-1078683.html

Deutscher Bundestag Wissenschaftliche Dienste. (2020). *Einzelfragen zu den Kosten eines Medizinstudiums (WD 8 - 3000 - 020/20)*. Retrieved January 5, 2025, from https://www.bundestag.de/resource/blob/702380/4582a586f8639efa3edf4a949b112c1f/WD-8-020-20-pdf-data.pdf

Docquier, F. (2014). The brain-drain from developing countries. *IZA World of Labor*. https://doi.org/10.15185/izawol.31

Docquier, F., & Rapoport, H. (2012). Globalization, brain-drain, and development. *Journal of Economic Literature, 50*(3), 681–730. https://doi.org/10.1257/jel.50.3.681

Docquier, F., & Rapoport, H. (2016). The brain-drain. In M. Vernengo, E. P. Caldentey, & B. J. Rosser Jr. (Eds.), *The New Palgrave Dictionary of Economics* (pp. 1–6). Palgrave Macmillan.

Dodani, S., & LaPorte, R. E. (2005). Brain-drain from developing countries: How can brain-drain be converted into wisdom gain? *Journal of the Royal Society of Medicine, 98*(11), 487–491. https://doi.org/10.1177/014107680509801107

Durmaz, A. (2022). Diaspora as a source of human capital: The effects of the relationship between scientific Turkish diaspora and the homeland on reverse brain-drain. *Migration and Development, 11*(3), 717–736. https://doi.org/10.1080/21632324.2020.1816036

Elmacıoğlu, L. (2021, November 21). Hekimler göçünün gözde ülkesi Almanya: Türkiye'den gidenler neden burayı tercih ediyor? *Independent Türkçe*. Retrieved January 15, 2025, from https://www.indyturk.com/node/431251/sa%C4%9Flik/hekimler-g%C3%B6%C3%A7%C3%BCn%C3%BCn-g%C3%B6zde-%C3%BClkesi-almanya-t%C3%BCrkiyeden-gidenler-neden-buray%C4%B1-tercih

Elveren, A. Y. (2018). *Brain-drain and gender inequality in Turkey*. Springer.

Erdem, A. K. (2022, July 4). 8 yılda 18 bin 685 yabancı sağlık çalışanı Türkiye'de çalışmaya başladı: Yabancılar, yurt dışına giden Türk sağlık çalışanlarının yerini doldurabilir mi? *Independent Türkçe*. Retrieved January 20, 2025, from https://www.indyturk.com/node/528146/sa%C4%9Flik/8-y%C4%B1lda-18-bin-685-yabanc%C4%B1-sa%C4%9Fl%C4%B1k-%C3%A7al%C4%B1%C5%9Fan%C4%B1-t%C3%BCrkiyede-%C3%A7al%C4%B1%C5%9Fmaya-ba%C5%9Flad%C4%B1-yabanc%C4%B1lar

Eser, E., Cil, E., Sen Gundogan, N. E., Col, M., Yildirim Ozturk, E. N., Thomas, D. T., et al. (2024). Push and pull factors of why medical students want to leave Türkiye: A countrywide multicenter study. *Teaching and Learning in Medicine, 36*(5), 588–600. https://doi.org/10.1080/10401334.2023.2229810

Faist, T. (1998). International migration and transnational social spaces: Their evolution, significance and future prospects. *InIIS-Arbeitspapier, 9*, 1–40.

Feld, S. (2021). *International migration, remittances and brain-drain*. Springer International Publishing.

Giannoccolo, P. (2009). *The brain-drain: A survey of the literature*. Università degli Studi di Milano-Bicocca, Department of Statistics, Working Paper (2006-03), 02. https://doi.org/10.2139/ssrn.1374329

Güngör, N. D., & Tansel, A. (2008). Brain-drain from Turkey: An investigation of students' return intentions. *Applied Economics, 40*(23), 3069–3087. https://doi.org/10.1080/00036840600993999

Güngör, N. D., & Tansel, A. (2014). Brain-drain from Turkey: Return intentions of skilled migrants. *International Migration, 52*(5), 208–226. https://doi.org/10.1111/imig.12013

Gürak, H. (2003). Hidden costs of technology transfer in the new age of imperialism: Adverse impacts of package deals with restrictive clauses. *YK Economic Review*, June, 1–27. Revisited in March 2025.

Gürak, H. (2009). Küreselleşme. Retrieved March 20, 2025, from https://www.academia.edu/29706776/K%C3%9CRESELLE%C5%9EME_Prof_Dr_Ay%C5%9Fe_%C4%B0rmi%C5%9Fin_katk%C4%B1lar%C4%B1yla

Gürak, H. (2024a). Plundering the skilled workforce. *World Review of Political Economy, 15*(3), 406–421. https://www.jstor.org/stable/48812984

Gürak, H. (2024b). *The economic value of creative mental labor: Economic growth and the labor theory of value*. Palgrave Macmillan.

Hopyar, Z. (2023). *Almanya'dan Türkiye'ye nitelikli geriye göç hareketi: Karar verme ve yeniden uyum süreçleri* [Unpublished doctoral dissertation, Sakarya Üniversitesi].

Hopyar, Z., Topal, F., & Tauscher, S. (2022). Diaspora kavramı ve Türkiye'nin diaspora politikasına yönelik üniversite öğrencilerinin algısı. *Journal of Political Administrative and Local Studies, 5*(1), 46–65.

Hussain, S. M. (2015). Reversing the brain-drain: Is it beneficial? *World Development, 67*, 310–322. https://doi.org/10.1016/j.worlddev.2014.10.023

Kalipeni, E., Semu, L. L., & Mbilizi, M. A. (2012). The brain-drain of health care professionals from sub-Saharan Africa: A geographic perspective. *Progress in Development Studies, 12*(2–3), 153–171. https://doi.org/10.1177/146499341101200305

Kamarulzaman, A., Ramnarayan, K., & Mocumbi, A. O. (2022). Plugging the medical brain-drain. *The Lancet, 400*(10362), 1492–1494. https://doi.org/10.1016/S0140-6736(22)02087-6

Keane, M. P., McCormick, B., & Popławska, G. (2020). Health care spending in the US vs UK: The roles of medical education costs, malpractice risk and defensive medicine. *European Economic Review, 124*, 103401. https://doi.org/10.1016/j.euroecorev.2020.103401

Kilic, O., Sonmez, E., Erzin, G., Guloksuz, S., & Pinto da Costa, M. (2019). Mobility trends of psychiatric trainees in Turkey: Hard to leave, harder to stay? *European Archives of Psychiatry and Clinical Neuroscience, 269*(1), 367–369. https://doi.org/10.1007/s00406-018-0914-2

Kılıçarslan, M. (2019). SWOT analysis of health tourism in Turkey. *Elektronik Sosyal Bilimler Dergisi, 18*(71), 135–145. https://doi.org/10.17755/esosder.467515

Kirigia, J. M., Gbary, A. R., Muthuri, L. K., Nyoni, J., & Seddoh, A. (2006). The cost of health professionals' brain-drain in Kenya. *BMC Health Services Research, 6*(89), 1–10. https://doi.org/10.1186/1472-6963-6-89

Kollar, E. (2013). Brain-drain. *International Encyclopedia of Ethics, 1–10.* https://doi.org/10.1002/9781444367072.wbiee873

Köser-Akçapar, S. (2006). Do brains really go down the drain? Highly skilled Turkish migrants in the USA and the "brain-drain" debate in Turkey. *Revue européenne des migrations internationales, 3*(3), 79–107. https://doi.org/10.4000/remi.3281

Kurnaz Ay, M., Sivri, B. B., Burggraf, L., Canbaz, M., Çelik, K., Çetiner, M. A., Çiftçi, A. M., Demirtürk, M., Eryiğit, U., Gehrmann, J., Kurt, Ş., Kunisch, R., Zehirlioğlu, L., Roos, M., & Aktürk, Z. (2024). Navigating Exodus: Understanding the Migration Dynamics of Health Care Professionals from Turkey. *European Journal of Humanities and Social Sciences, 4*(1), 48–58. https://doi.org/10.24018/ejsocial.2024.4.1.519

Kwok, V., & Leland, H. (1982). An economic model of the brain-drain. *The American Economic Review, 72*(1), 91–100.

Lu, X., & Zhang, W. (2015). The reversed brain-drain: A mixed-method study of the reversed migration of Chinese overseas scientists. *Science, Technology and Society, 20*(3), 279–299. https://doi.org/10.1177/0971721815597127

Marini, G., & Yang, L. (2021). Globally bred Chinese talents returning home: An analysis of a reverse brain-drain flagship policy. *Science and Public Policy, 48*(4), 541–552. https://doi.org/10.1093/scipol/scab021

Martin, P., Midgley, E., & Teitelbaum, M. (2001). Migration and development: Focus on Turkey. *International Migration Review, 35*, 596–605. https://doi.org/10.1111/j.1747-7379.2001.tb00031.x

Martineau, T., Decker, K., & Bundred, P. (2004). "Brain-drain" of health professionals: From rhetoric to responsible action. *Health Policy, 70*(1), 1–10. https://doi.org/10.1016/j.healthpol.2004.01.006

Mattoo, A., Neagu, I. C., & Özden, Ç. (2008). Brain waste? Educated immigrants in the US labor market. *Journal of Development Economics, 87*(2), 255–269. https://doi.org/10.1016/j.jdeveco.2007.05.001

McAuliffe, M., & Oucho, L. A. (2024). Report overview: Migration continues to be part of the solution in a rapidly changing world, but key challenges remain. In M. M. McAuliffe & L. A. Oucho (Eds.), *World Migration Report, 2024*(1).

International Organization for Migration (IOM). https://doi.org/10.1002/wom3.33
Metin, F. (2023). Brain-drain from Türkiye: Register evidence of non-returning graduates. *Research in Educational Administration and Leadership, 8*(2), 373–419. https://doi.org/10.30828/real.1149770
Mills, E. J., Kanters, S., Hagopian, A., Bansback, N., Nachega, J., Alberton, M., et al. (2011). The financial cost of doctors emigrating from sub-Saharan Africa: human capital analysis. *BMJ, 343.* https://doi.org/10.1136/bmj.d7031
Muula, A. S. (2005). Is there any solution to the "brain-drain" of health professionals and knowledge from Africa? *Croatian Medical Journal, 46*(1), 21–29.
OECD. (2023). *Health at a glance 2023.* OECD Publishing. Retrieved January 3, 2025, from https://www.oecd.org/content/dam/oecd/en/publications/reports/2023/11/health-at-a-glance-2023_e04f8239/7a7afb35-en.pdf
Oğuzkan, T. (1976). The scope and nature of Turkish brain-drain. In N. Abadan-Unat (Ed.), *Turkish workers in Europe, 1960–1975: A socio-economic reappraisal* (pp. 74–103). E. J. Brill.
Omay, E. G. G., & Cengiz, E. (2013). Health tourism in Turkey: Opportunities and threats. *Mediterranean Journal of Social Sciences, 4*(10), 424–434. https://doi.org/10.5901/mjss.2013.v4n10p424
Önal, F. G., & Akay, F. E. (2024). Are Turkish doctors in deep water? The role of professional ethics and factors affecting the medical brain-drain: A qualitative study from Turkey. *Developing World Bioethics, 24,* 284–295. https://doi.org/10.1111/dewb.12426
Opendoors. (n.d.). International students. Retrieved February 05, 2025, from https://opendoorsdata.org/data/international-students/
Oteiza, E. (1996). Brain-drain: An historical and conceptual framework. *International Scientific Migrations, Revista Redes, Universidad de Quilmes, 3*(7), 101–120.
Pang, T., Lansang, M. A., & Haines, A. (2002). Brain-drain and health professionals: A global problem needs global solutions. *BMJ, 324*(7336), 499–500.
Portes, A. (1976). Determinants of the brain-drain. *International Migration Review, 10*(4), 489–508.
Raghuram, P. (2009). Caring about 'brain-drain' migration in a postcolonial world. *Geoforum, 40*(1), 25–33. https://doi.org/10.1016/j.geoforum.2008.03.005
Ravenstein, E. G. (1885). *The laws of migration.* Royal Statistical Society.
Republic of Türkiye Ministry of Health. (2023a, December 22). *Hekimler özelden kamuya, yurt dışından Türkiye'ye dönüyor.* Türkiye Cumhuriyeti Sağlık Bakanlığı. Retrieved January 08, 2025, from https://www.saglik.gov.tr/TR-101413/hekimler-ozelden-kamuya-yurt-disindan-turkiyeye-donuyor.html#:~:text=Bakan%20Koca%2C%20payla%C5%9F%C4%B1m%C4%B1nda%20%C5%9Funlar%C4%B1%20kaydetti,de%2028%20hekim%20geri%20d%C3%B6nd%C3%BC

Republic of Türkiye Ministry of Health. (2023b, September 06). *Kamuya dönen hekim sayısı 8 bini buldu*. Türkiye Cumhuriyeti Sağlık Bakanlığı. Retrieved January 09, 2025, from https://www.saglik.gov.tr/TR-99358/kamuya-donen-hekim-sayisi-8-bini-buldu.html

Republic of Türkiye Ministry of Health. (2023c, August 01). *Sağlıkta ikinci beyaz reform dönemi başladı*. Türkiye Cumhuriyeti Sağlık Bakanlığı. Retrieved February 22, 2025, from https://www.saglik.gov.tr/TR%2C96882/saglikta-ikinci-beyaz-reform-donemi-basladi.html?utm_source

Rizvi, F. (2005). Rethinking "brain-drain" in the era of globalisation. *Asia Pacific Journal of Education, 25*(2), 175–192. https://doi.org/10.1080/02188790500337965

Sanchez-Montijano, E., Kaya, A., & Sökmen, M. J. (2018). Highly skilled migration between the EU and Turkey: Drivers and scenarios. *FEUTURE Online Paper, 21*. Retrieved January 21, 2025, from https://eu.bilgi.edu.tr/media/files/Skilled_Migration_between_Turkey_and_the_EU_by_Sanchez_Kaya_and_S%C3%B6kmen.pdf

Şen Olgay, S., & Yurt, S. (2023). Türkiye'den İngiltere'ye göç eden sağlık çalışanlarının göç nedenleri ve yaşam doyumlarının belirlenmesi. *Sağlık ve Hemşirelik Yönetimi Dergisi, 10*(1), 99–107. https://doi.org/10.54304/shyd.2023.60565

Serour, G. I. (2009). Healthcare workers and the brain-drain. *International Journal of Gynecology & Obstetrics, 106*(2), 175–178. https://doi.org/10.1016/j.ijgo.2009.03.035

Tannock, S. (2007). *Beyond national borders: Reframing the global brain-drain debate*. SKOPE Research Paper No. 73. Cardiff University.

Tauscher, S., & Eskicioglu, Y. C. (2025). Media, imperialism, and ideology: US partisan media's discursive approach to Latin America and the Middle East. *Middle East Critique, 34*(4), 749–770. https://doi.org/10.1080/19436149.2025.2496846

Tezcan, T. (2018). On the move in search of health and care: Circular migration and family conflict amongst older Turkish immigrants in Germany. *Journal of Aging Studies, 46*, 82–92. https://doi.org/10.1016/j.jaging.2018.07.001

TÜBİTAK. (2013, October 21). *Tersine beyin göçü meyvelerini veriyor*. TÜBİTAK. Retrieved February 4, 2025, from https://tubitak.gov.tr/tr/haber/tersine-beyin-gocu-meyvelerini-veriyor

TÜBİTAK. (2015, May 14). *TÜBİTAK'ın "Tersine Beyin Göçü Programı" başarıya ulaştı*. TÜBİTAK. Retrieved February 4, 2025, from https://tubitak.gov.tr/tr/haber/tubitakin-tersine-beyin-gocu-programi-basariya-ulasti

TÜBİTAK. (2021, March 17). *TÜBİTAK'tan tersine beyin göçü için 2. çağrı*. TÜBİTAK. Retrieved February 5, 2025, from https://tubitak.gov.tr/tr/haber/tubitaktan-tersine-beyin-gocu-icin-2-cagri,

TÜİK. (2024a, July 19). *Uluslararası göç istatistikleri, 2023*. Türkiye İstatistik Kurumu. Retrieved January 13, 2025, from https://data.tuik.gov.tr/Bulten/Index?p=Uluslararasi-Goc-Istatistikleri-2023-53544

TÜİK. (2024b, September 26). *Yükseköğretim beyin göçü istatistikleri, 2021–2023*. Türkiye İstatistik Kurumu. https://data.tuik.gov.tr/Bulten/Index?p=Yuksekogretim-Beyin-Gocu-Istatistikleri-2021-2023-53839#:~:text=Y%C3%BCksek%C3%B6%C4%9Fretim%20mezunlar%C4%B1n%C4%B1n%20beyin%20g%C3%B6%C3%A7%C3%BC%20oran%C4%B1,%252%2C4%20olarak%20ger%C3%A7ekle%C5%9Fti, Retrieved 2025.01.13

Turkish Medical Association—Türk Tabipleri Birliği [@ttborgtr]. (2023, December 29). TTB'ye "İyi Hal Belgesi" başvuru sayısı; Aralık ayında 240, 2023 yılında 3025 oldu. [Thumbnail with link attached] [Tweet]. Twitter. Retrieved January 5, 2025, from https://x.com/ttborgtr/status/1740746140457279822

Uğur, N. (2022). Great risk for education cost: Brain-drain (Resident physicians case). *STED, 31*(2), 115–122. https://doi.org/10.17942/sted.979463

Ulupinar, S., Şen, Y., & Eycan, Ö. (2024). Original research: Nurses' attitudes toward brain-drain and the associated factors. *The American Journal of Nursing, 124*(3), 22–32. https://doi.org/10.1097/01.NAJ.0001007672.35687.2d

Wächter, B. (2006). Brain-drain: What we know and what we do not know. In U. Teichler (Ed.), *The formative years of scholars* (pp. 51–66). Portland Press.

Wadhwa, V. (2009). A reverse brain-drain. *Issues in Science and Technology, 25*(3), 45–52.

Wallerstein, I. (2020). *World-systems analysis: An introduction*. Duke University Press.

World Bank. (2024). *World Development Report 2024: The middle-income trap*. : The World Bank. Retrieved January 10, 2025, from https://datacatalog.worldbank.org/search/dataset/0037712

YÖK. (n.d.). Yükseköğretim Kurulu Tarafından Eğitim ve Öğretime Başlanması ve Sürdürülebilmesi İçin Asgari Koşulları Belirlenen Programlar. Retrieved January 3, 2025, from https://www.yok.gov.tr/kurumsal/idari-birimler/egitim-ogretim-dairesi/asgari-kosullar

Yüksel, Z., (2024, October 20). *Endişe veren tablo! Beyin göçü neden artıyor?* Haber Global. Retrieved January 15, 2025, from https://haberglobal.com.tr/amp/yazarlar/endise-veren-tablo-beyin-gocu-neden-artiyor-387999

Zweig, D. (2006). Competing for talent: China's strategies to reverse the brain-drain. *Int'l Lab. Rev., 145*, 65–90. https://doi.org/10.1111/j.1564-913X.2006.tb00010.x

CHAPTER 4

On the Emigration of Engineers and Technicians

Haşmet Gökirmak and Fuat Sekmen

... [the rain clouds] go wherever you want; your kharaj (land tax) will come to me!"
—Harun al-Rashid, the fifth Abbasid Caliph

Introduction

Harun al-Rashid, the fifth Abbasid Caliph,[1] once remarked to the rain clouds, "Go wherever you want; your kharaj (land tax) will come to me." This statement reflects that well-educated professionals from distant lands

[1] Harun al-Rashid, born in 763 CE and died in 809 CE, was the fifth Abbasid Caliph, reigning from 786 to 809 CE. He is one of the most prominent and legendary rulers in Islamic history, particularly remembered for the cultural, scientific, and economic flourishing of the Islamic Golden Age under his rule.

H. Gökirmak (✉)
Department of Business and Management Sciences, Istanbul Sabahattin Zaim University, İstanbul, Turkey
e-mail: hasmet.gokirmak@izu.edu.tr

H. Gürak (ed.), *The Economics of Migration of Highly Skilled Workers from Türkiye*,
https://doi.org/10.1007/978-3-032-10606-3_4

ultimately come to contribute to developed countries that wield economic control and political influence.

Brain drain is the migration of well-educated, qualified, and talented individuals from underdeveloped or developing countries to more developed ones. This phenomenon often arises from inadequate opportunities, unemployment, or the inability to practice their profession as desired in less developed countries (LDCs). The term "brain drain" is used because these highly skilled individuals take their knowledge and experience with them when they leave. Brain drain signifies the permanent transfer of intellect and knowledge from one country to another, implying that well-equipped and competent individuals are leaving their home country (Savunma Sanayii Dergilik, 2022).

Brain drain is not a phenomenon that has emerged only in contemporary times. It dates back to when people began to gather in settlements called cities. In ancient times, as the political power of a particular country weakened and signs of collapse and ruin intensified, scholars, artists, and thinkers who had gathered around its palaces or scientific institutions felt the need to seek new markets. As a result, the palaces and scientific centers of newly emerging, stronger countries poised to replace the declining civilization became a refuge and source of support for such individuals (Kuşçu, 1979, p. 4).

Several studies have classified the factors influencing migration decisions into three levels: societal-level (macro) studies explain migration trends as part of a country's social, political, and economic development; household-level (meso) studies link migration to household or community factors based on social ties and networks; and individual-level (micro) studies focus on personal values, desires, and the cost-benefit analysis of potential immigrants. At the macro level, Dudu and Rojo (2022, p. 141) categorize the characteristics of migration destinations into four groups: security-based, labor market, social, and geographic drivers (Fig. 4.1).

F. Sekmen
Faculty of Political Science-Department of Economics, Sakarya University, Sakarya, Turkey
e-mail: sekmen@sakarya.edu.tr

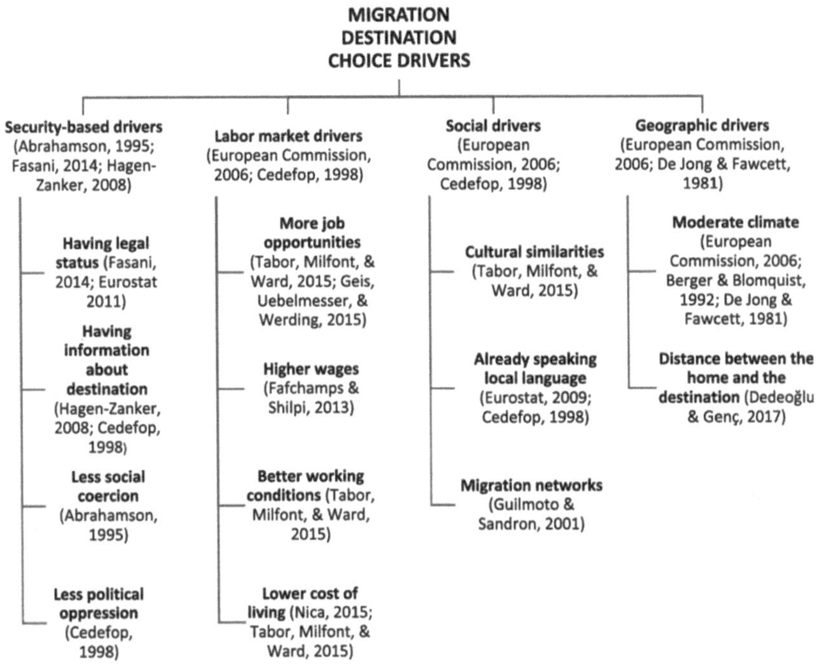

Fig. 4.1 Drivers of migration destination. (Source: Dudu & Rojo, 2022, [Figure 1, p. 141])

Background on Emigration Trends in Türkiye

According to the World Bank (2025), Türkiye is the 17th largest economy in the world, with a GDP of $1.32 trillion as of 2024. The country is a member of the OECD and the G20 and has become an increasingly significant donor of official development assistance (ODA).

From 2006 to 2017, Türkiye implemented ambitious reforms and experienced high growth rates, elevating it to upper-middle-income and significantly reducing poverty. Between 2002 and 2022, Türkiye's real gross domestic product (GDP) growth averaged 5.4%, resulting in more than a doubling of income per capita (in real terms) over the same period while reducing the poverty rate from over 20% in 2007 to 7.6% in 2021 (World Bank, 2025).

However, the country has experienced a significant brain drain over the past decade. Many highly skilled professionals, such as doctors, engineers, and technicians, left the country for various reasons. Figure 4.2 illustrates the number of people who emigrated from Türkiye between 2019 and 2024. In 2024, about 150,000 people, many high-tech professionals, left Türkiye.

Emerging markets and developing economies, which often depend on manual labor and traditional industries, might initially experience fewer disruptions from advanced technologies. However, they may also miss out on the productivity benefits of advanced technologies due to inadequate infrastructure and a lack of highly skilled workers. Over time, this technological gap could worsen existing economic inequalities as advanced economies use advanced technologies to gain a competitive edge while emerging markets and developing economies struggle to incorporate advanced technologies into their growth strategies (Cazzaniga et al., 2024, pp. 21).

Engineers and technicians have also been part of this emigration trend. Political uncertainties and economic difficulties in Türkiye have motivated many to migrate to more stable countries offering better professional growth. While Türkiye continues to produce highly skilled professionals, the emigration trend highlights the need for improved domestic possibilities and working conditions to keep these valuable talents (Akın & Karadaş, 2023, pp. 2).

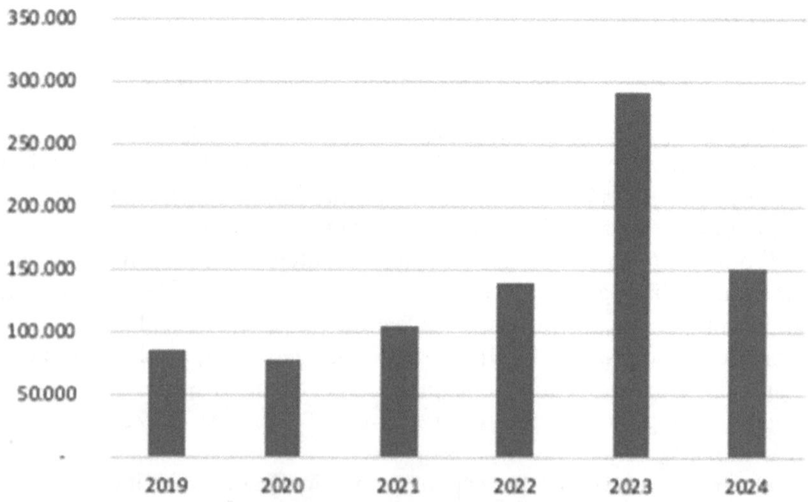

Fig. 4.2 Emigration from Türkiye. (TÜİK, 2024)

Importance of Engineers and Technicians to the Turkish Economy

Engineers and technicians are vital to the Turkish economy due to their significant contributions in various sectors. These professionals lead technological advancements, nurture innovation, and increase productivity, making Turkish industries more competitive globally. They are instrumental in attracting investments and creating highly skilled jobs, which helps retain talent within the country. They contribute to economic diversification and export growth in sectors like ICT, AI, and advanced manufacturing, and improve Türkiye's trade balance and economic position. Their expertise is vital for the digital transformation of businesses and public services, improving efficiency and customer satisfaction. Additionally, their work in research and development (R&D) centers stimulates innovation, attracts international partnerships, and obtains funding, helping to make Türkiye a regional hub for technological innovation. These professionals also play a critical role in carrying out Industry 4.0 practices, driving economic growth, and developing sustainable technologies that support long-term economic sustainability and environmental protection (Eurostat, 2024).

This chapter examines the emigration trends of engineers and technicians from Türkiye over the past ten years. The financial and alternative costs associated with their education are analyzed. The educational costs and economic impacts of the brain drain phenomenon in Türkiye are explored by analyzing migration data. The financial cost of education in less developed countries (LDCs) and the alternative cost of this education in host countries are assessed to highlight the economic impact for home and destination countries. The findings aim to inform policymakers of the need for strategic interventions to mitigate the adverse effects of highly skilled labor migration and enhance the retention of critical talent within Türkiye.

Literature Review

Overview of Brain Drain Theories

Brain drain, or human capital flight, is the emigration of highly skilled and educated individuals from one country to another for better career opportunities, higher salaries, improved living conditions, and political stability. Brain drain is influenced by push factors such as political instability, lack of job opportunities, and poor working conditions in the home countries. Brain drain pull factors in the host countries include higher wages and advanced research opportunities. The economic impact on home countries includes a significant loss of human capital, slower economic growth, reduced government revenues due to the reduced tax base, and the underutilization of skills, known as "brain waste." Conversely, destination countries benefit from acquiring highly skilled labor, which fills critical gaps in sectors like technology and healthcare, drives innovation, enhances productivity, and contributes to economic dynamism through cultural and economic integration. However, challenges like labor market integration and competition with native workers may arise. Home countries can create attractive local opportunities, engage with their diaspora for knowledge transfer and investments, implement policy reforms to address the root causes of emigration, and focus on education and training to replenish lost human capital to mitigate brain drain.

The mobility of highly qualified workers has been explained by two main theories: dependency theory and modernization theory (Aydın, 2012, pp. 204–205). Dependency theory views this mobility as a form of exploitation by the global market, arguing that Western-dominated market structures keep developing countries economically and politically dependent. It highlights how rich industrialized countries recruit highly skilled professionals from developing countries, exacerbating underdevelopment and poverty. Proponents of this theory, like Indian economist Bhagwati, propose international regulation and financial compensation for sending countries, such as a brain drain tax.

In contrast, modernization theory positively sees highly skilled worker migration as part of a free global labor market governed by supply and demand. It suggests that highly skilled workers should utilize their abilities where they are most efficient and argues that government interventions in migration would distort international competition and global welfare. This theory relates the emigration of highly skilled workers to insufficient job opportunities and the overproduction of scientific elites in developing countries.

Both theories recognize wage imbalances, living standards, immigration programs, and political circumstances as drivers of migration, but they often overlook subjective motives like self-realization and autonomy. The brain drain discussions are criticized for focusing mainly on economic impacts, methodological nationalism, and neglecting the socioeconomic advantages for emigrants.

The transnational migration perspective changes this view by seeing migration as an ongoing movement, creating "transnational spaces" that mix parts of both the home and new countries. It suggests looking at these mixed spaces between Germany and Türkiye.

Since the 1990s, a new perspective has appeared that considers the positive effects of highly skilled migration for sending and receiving countries, highlighting diaspora networks, the return of migrants, and corporate networks as positive outcomes. This approach highlights the role of internal labor markets in aiding the mobility of highly qualified workers (Aydın, 2012, pp. 204–207).

The study by Marzook et al. (2023) looks at the problem of IT professionals leaving Sri Lanka. They argue that the reasons for the emigration of these professionals are complex and have a significant impact on the country's economy and technological development. The research finds that these professionals leave mainly because of limited career opportunities, low wages, poor infrastructure, and political instability. On the other hand, attractive job opportunities, higher salaries, better work-life balance, and advanced technology in different countries encourage them to leave. This brain drain has profound effects, as Sri Lanka loses highly skilled people who could help the country's economic growth and technological progress. It also erodes the IT industry and makes Sri Lanka less competitive globally (Marzook et al., 2023, pp. 168).

To solve this problem, the authors suggest that the government improve IT infrastructure, promote research and development, and encourage cooperation between universities and industries. The government, private sector, and educational institutions should work together to improve IT education, match it with industry needs, and encourage entrepreneurship. These steps will help create a robust IT environment that keeps and attracts highly skilled professionals. The study concludes that a comprehensive approach is needed to reduce brain drain and help Sri Lanka become a global IT hub.

Previous Studies on Highly Skilled Labor Emigration from Türkiye

Host countries benefit significantly from the arrival of highly skilled professionals who boost innovation, productivity, and economic growth. These professionals fill essential skill gaps in technology and engineering. Turkish emigrants' different backgrounds and experiences help spark new ideas and creativity in host countries, making them more competitive globally (Kirişçi, 2007, pp. 2).

Many young, well-educated, and highly skilled professionals from Türkiye, especially in engineering, IT, and AI, are leaving the country. Better job opportunities, political stability, and a higher quality of life in other countries attract them. These professionals significantly contribute to their new countries' economies and innovation capabilities. It is important to address why they emigrate to keep talented people from leaving and lessen the adverse effects on Türkiye's economy.

Gürak (1990) framed the brain drain not merely as a consequence of individual career decisions but as a systemic and geopolitical mechanism of resource extraction. Gürak argues that the emigration of highly skilled professionals from Türkiye constitutes an economic loss and a strategic erosion of national intellectual capacity. He conceptualizes this phenomenon as a form of "intellectual desertification," warning that continued human capital flight weakens the developmental foundations of source countries. In another widely cited commentary, Gürak emphasizes that "the brain drain from developing to developed countries represents the largest form of resource transfer, for which no compensation is provided." This viewpoint underscores the asymmetric nature of global labor mobility, where developed nations benefit from the educational investments of poorer countries without bearing the associated costs. Gürak's structuralist interpretation enriches the theoretical debate by positioning brain drain as both a symptom and a driver of global inequality, calling for a more just and reciprocal framework in managing highly skilled migration flows (Gürak, 1990, pp. 123–125).

In a critical reflection on globalization and its socioeconomic ramifications, Gürak (2008) underscores the asymmetric structure of the global economic order, which systematically channels human capital from the periphery to the core. He argues that globalization, far from being an inclusive and neutral process, often exacerbates inequalities between countries by enabling developed nations to benefit from developing economies' intellectual and professional resources. Within this framework, the emigration of highly skilled professionals—especially from countries like Türkiye—is not merely a byproduct of market forces but an institutionalized mechanism of capital extraction. Gürak's analysis highlights how global integration without safeguards for source countries can result in a sustained "intellectual expropriation," weakening national innovation systems and undermining long-term development strategies. His approach contributes to the structuralist and dependency theory literature by framing brain drain as an embedded consequence of the uneven dynamics of globalization.

Gürak (2024, pp. 408) critiques the systemic mechanisms through which developed countries attract and absorb highly skilled labor from developing economies. His analysis situates this trend within a broader framework of global inequality and structural dependence, characterizing it as a form of "modern plunder" that exacerbates underdevelopment in sending countries. Drawing on political economy and institutional perspectives, Gürak emphasizes that losing highly educated professionals, particularly in STEM, undermines the fiscal capacity and human capital accumulation of countries like Türkiye. He argues that without international regulatory mechanisms or compensatory arrangements, this asymmetrical flow of talent perpetuates a cycle of dependency and deprives origin countries of the very workforce they have invested in through public education and national development programs. Gürak's perspective adds a critical dimension to existing migration literature by underscoring the geopolitical and distributive consequences of highly skilled emigration, reinforcing the need for a more equitable global governance framework for labor mobility.

Economic Contributions of Highly Skilled Migrants in Host Countries

Highly skilled migrants significantly improve the economies of the countries they move to in many ways. They fill essential job openings in healthcare, technology, engineering, and education, which helps businesses and public services run smoothly and support economic growth. Their different experiences and knowledge lead to new ideas and increased productivity, which also allows local workers. Highly skilled migrants are crucial in research and development, pushing technological and scientific progress forward. Many become entrepreneurs, creating jobs, introducing new products, and stimulating economic activity. Their higher employment rates and wages result in substantial tax contributions, funding public services, and addressing demographic challenges by sustaining social security systems.

Additionally, highly skilled migrants contribute to cultural diversity, leading to more dynamic and creative work environments, translating into innovative business practices and enhanced customer service. Their economic integration through labor market participation and spending supports local businesses and stimulates growth. Examples from countries like the United States, Germany, the UK, Canada, and Türkiye illustrate how highly skilled migrants are critical to filling labor shortages, driving innovation, and fostering economic dynamism (Kirişçi, 2007, pp. 2).

Case Studies and Evidence

- **The United States**: Research shows that immigrants are critical to the U.S. economy, particularly in STEM fields, where they constitute a significant portion of the workforce. They have been pivotal in Silicon Valley's tech boom and driving innovations across various sectors.
- **European Union**: In countries like Germany and the UK, highly skilled migrants have been essential in addressing labor shortages in healthcare and engineering. They have also contributed to academic research, with many universities relying on international faculty and researchers.
- **Canada**: Canada's immigration policy has focused on attracting highly skilled migrants to support economic growth. These migrants have played a crucial role in the tech sector, with cities like Toronto and Vancouver becoming hubs for technology and innovation due to the influx of highly skilled professionals.
- **Türkiye**: Syrian migrants have made substantial contributions to the Turkish economy, impacting various sectors positively. Approximately 14,000 companies have been established by Syrians, significantly boosting economic activity. In 2017, the economic activities of Syrian refugees contributed about 1.96% to Türkiye's GDP, with projections indicating this could increase to 4% by 2028. Their involvement in the labor market, primarily in the informal sector, has filled crucial labor gaps and led to an estimated increase in production across different sectors (Hardan, 2024). Furthermore, Syrian entrepreneurs have demonstrated strong entrepreneurial capabilities, with the number of Syrian-owned businesses increasing by 168% between 2014 and 2016. Syrian-owned businesses, mainly concentrated in cities like Gaziantep, have created jobs and stimulated local economies.
- Additionally, Turkish companies have benefited from reduced social security contributions when employing Syrians, enhancing overall economic efficiency. Integrating Syrian refugees into the Turkish economy has led to direct and indirect benefits, including increased

production, job creation, and entrepreneurial activity. Their economic contributions will increase if their employment opportunities, education, and entrepreneurial support improve.

Analysis of Emigration Trends

Several studies have examined why highly skilled workers leave Türkiye and the effects of their departure. The study by Dedeoğlu and Genç (2017, pp. 7) employs a gravity model to investigate the factors influencing the emigration of Turkish professionals to 31 European countries from 1960 to 2013. The analysis, using various estimation strategies, finds that economic, demographic, and cultural factors significantly impact the migration decisions to these destination countries.

Historically, Turkish emigration began in the 1960s, primarily due to labor recruitment agreements with European countries like Germany. This initial wave mainly consisted of low-skilled workers. However, since the 2000s, there has been a notable increase in the emigration of highly skilled professionals, including engineers, IT specialists, and academics.

The stock of Turkish migrants (based on country of birth) in EU member states has been rising since 1960 (UNDESA, 2017; World Bank, 2011). By 2017, 2,668,826 people from Türkiye lived in the EU-28 (see Fig. 4.3), with over 1.5 million residing in Germany alone.

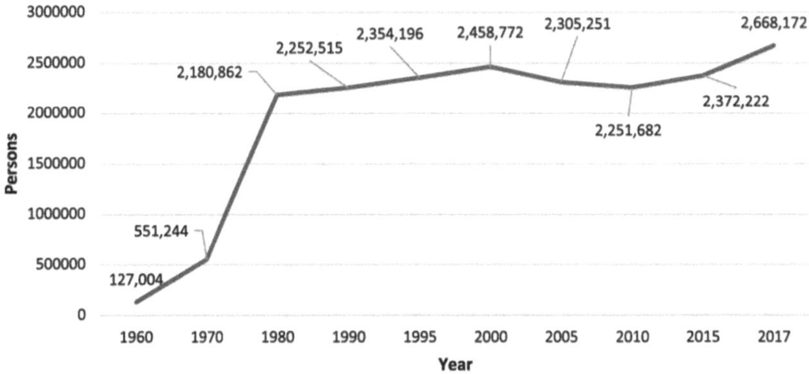

Fig. 4.3 Turkish migration stock in the EU-28. (Source: For 1960–1980: World Bank [2017])

Historical Trends in the Emigration of Engineers and Technicians from Türkiye

Over the past few decades, the emigration trends of low-skilled labor and highly skilled professionals, including engineers and technicians from Türkiye, have shown significant fluctuations influenced by various economic, political, and social factors.

Early Emigration Trends (1960s–1990s)
1960s–1970s:

- **Labor Migration**: During the 1960s, Turkish migration was primarily labor-driven, with many workers moving to Western Europe, especially Germany, under labor recruitment agreements. During the 1970s, however, Turkish immigrants to Europe were equally motivated by political and economic factors due to conflict between the political left and right. This period saw a significant outflow of less-skilled labor, but some highly skilled professionals, including engineers and technicians, also emigrated to seek better opportunities (Kirişçi, 2007, pp. 91; Dudu & Rojo, 2022, pp. 145).

1980s–1990s:

- **Political Instability and Economic Challenges**: The political instability and economic challenges of the 1980s, including the 1980 military coup and economic downturns, prompted many highly skilled professionals to emigrate. Engineers and technicians sought stable job opportunities abroad, particularly in Europe and North America (Kirişçi, 2007, pp. 93; Dudu & Rojo, 2022, pp. 145).

Late 1990s to Early 2000s
Late 1990s:

- **Economic Reforms and EU Prospects:** In the late 1990s, Türkiye made economic reforms and had the possibility of joining the European Union. This temporarily slowed down the emigration rate. However, ongoing economic problems still drove some highly skilled professionals to seek opportunities abroad (Tuncel, 2021).

Early 2000s:

- **Growth of the IT Sector:** The global IT sector grew in the early 2000s, affecting the emigration patterns of Turkish engineers. Many Turkish professionals moved to countries like the United States, Canada, and the EU, with a high demand for tech talent. More engineers and technicians relocated during this period for better career prospects and higher salaries abroad (Tuncel, 2021).

Post-2010 Trends
2010–2015:

- **Economic Growth and Political Stability:** Türkiye experienced strong economic growth and relative political stability, which slowed the emigration of professionals. During this period, many engineers and technicians found plenty of opportunities within Türkiye, reducing the need to leave the country (Dudu & Rojo, 2022, pp. 141).

Post-2016:

- **Increased Emigration due to Political and Economic Turmoil**: After the attempted coup in 2016, the resulting political instability and economic challenges significantly increased the emigration rate of highly skilled professionals. Many engineers and technicians left Türkiye to find opportunities in more politically stable and economically prosperous countries (Dudu & Rojo, 2022, pp. 146).

Recent Trends (2020s)
2020–2023:

- **COVID-19 Pandemic and Economic Uncertainty**: The COVID-19 pandemic and its economic effects aggravated the emigration trend. Many highly skilled professionals faced job insecurity and economic hardships, prompting them to seek opportunities abroad. The ongoing political and economic instability continued to drive engineers and technicians to leave Türkiye (Dudu & Rojo, 2022, pp. 146).

The historical trends in the emigration of highly skilled professionals from Türkiye show a complex mix of economic, political, and social factors. In some periods, economic growth and political stability have slowed emigration, while periods of instability and economic challenges have significantly increased the outflow of highly skilled workers. Understanding these trends is crucial for developing policies to keep experienced workers and reduce the negative impacts of brain drain on Türkiye's economy.

Demographic and Professional Profiles of Emigrants from Türkiye

The impact of this brain drain on Türkiye is significant. The loss of highly skilled labor slows innovation and economic growth and reduces the country's ability to compete globally. It also affects critical sectors such as technology and education, vital for the country's development.

The emigration of highly skilled professionals from Türkiye involves various demographics and professions, motivated by economic opportunities, political stability, and quality of life. Key reasons for this trend include economic instability, political uncertainties, and the search for better career prospects abroad. Studies show that the migration of highly skilled workers from Türkiye has increased due to political issues and economic hardship after the 2016 attempted coup and subsequent government actions. These factors have pushed many professionals to seek more stable and prosperous environments in Europe, the United States, and Canada.

Efforts to mitigate the brain drain include improving local job opportunities, political reforms, and engaging with the diaspora to facilitate knowledge transfer and investment. However, the trend of highly skilled emigration continues to pose challenges for Türkiye's long-term economic and social development.

Most recent emigrants are young professionals, predominantly within the 25–40 age range. This demographic typically includes recent graduates and early to mid-career professionals seeking better opportunities abroad (Elveren, 2018, pp. 64). Although traditionally male-dominated, recent trends show an increasing number of female professionals emigrating. However, men still constitute the majority, particularly in technical fields like engineering and IT (Elveren, 2018, pp. 64). Emigrants often possess high educational qualifications, including bachelor's, master's, and Ph.D. degrees in engineering, computer science, and information technology.

Engineers across various specializations, such as civil, mechanical, electrical, and software engineering, represent a significant portion of the emigrant population. They are drawn to international opportunities offering advanced career prospects and higher salaries (Kirişçi, 2007).

Highly skilled technicians, especially those in high-tech industries, emigrate for better job security, advanced technology, and professional growth opportunities (Tuncel, 2021, pp. 3).

Many emigrants are early to mid-career professionals with 3–10 years of experience. This highly mobile group seeks international exposure to enhance their skills and career trajectories (Kirişçi, 2007). Although less common, senior professionals with significant experience and expertise also emigrate, often taking up leadership roles or specialized positions in multinational companies and research institutions.

Push and Pull Factors Influencing Emigration from Türkiye

The emigration of highly skilled professionals from Türkiye is driven by push factors (negative aspects that drive individuals to leave) and pull factors (positive aspects that attract individuals to other countries). Understanding these factors is vital for developing strategies to keep talent and mitigate brain drain. By addressing the underlying issues, Türkiye can create a more stable and appealing environment for highly skilled professionals, helping to promote innovation, economic growth, and global competitiveness.

Push Factors

Qualified professionals are leaving Türkiye because of economic instability, political uncertainty, limited career opportunities, lower quality of life, social and cultural pressures, and the pursuit of better educational opportunities. These factors push highly skilled individuals to seek better conditions and opportunities in other countries.

Economic Instability

1. **High Inflation and Unemployment**: Economic instability, with high inflation and unemployment rates, makes it difficult for professionals to find stable and well-paying jobs in Türkiye. This uncertainty causes many professionals to look for better opportunities in other countries (Dudu & Rojo, 2022, pp. 146).

2. **Limited Career Advancement**: Professionals in Türkiye often have limited chances for career growth. The absence of clear career paths, insufficient funding for research, and a lack of support for innovation drive them to look for better opportunities in more developed countries (Tuncel, 2021).

Political and Social Factors

1. **Political Instability**: Political instability, restrictions on freedom of expression, and concerns about democracy make qualified professionals feel insecure, leading them to leave Türkiye. Frequent changes in government policies create an unpredictable environment. Events such as the 2016 attempted coup and subsequent political turmoil have led many to seek stability and security in other countries (Dudu & Rojo, 2022, pp. 143).
2. **Lack of Freedom and Rights**: Concerns over freedom of expression, press freedom, and human rights issues have also driven emigration. Professionals, particularly those in academia and media, often feel constrained and prefer environments where they can work and express themselves freely.
3. **Social and Cultural Factors**: Social pressures, including issues related to gender equality and human rights, along with a desire for greater personal freedoms, influence the decision to emigrate.

Quality of Life

1. **Healthcare and Education**: Lower living standards, concerns about public services, and dissatisfaction with healthcare and education systems motivate individuals to emigrate for improved quality of life. Pursuing higher-quality education and advanced training abroad is significant as professionals seek to enhance their qualifications and skills in more developed academic environments. Inadequate healthcare services and limited educational opportunities for their children prompt many professionals to move to countries with better public services (Kirişçi, 2007, pp. 92).
2. **Safety and Security**: Personal safety and security concerns due to political unrest or high crime rates can drive individuals to emigrate. A safer living environment strongly motivates families to consider relocation.

Pull Factors

Countries within the European Union, such as Germany and other developed Western nations like the United States, compete globally to attract highly skilled migrants. For instance, the European Union implemented the "Blue Card" system in 2009 to attract highly qualified individuals. In Germany, regulatory conditions are continually being relaxed to promote the migration of highly skilled and educated professionals. Structurally, this phenomenon presents a dual aspect. While the conditions for emigration from Türkiye remain stringent, contemporary global dynamics reveal that countries that seek to limit migration in various forms establish highly facilitative mechanisms simultaneously to attract highly skilled migrants.

Economic Opportunities

1. **Higher Salaries and Better Job Prospects**: Developed countries often offer higher salaries and better job prospects, especially in high-demand fields such as IT, engineering, and AI. The promise of financial stability and career growth is a significant pull factor (Dudu & Rojo, 2022).
2. **Entrepreneurial Support**: Countries that provide robust support for entrepreneurs, including access to funding, mentorship, and a supportive business environment, attract highly skilled professionals looking to start their ventures (Tuncel, 2021).

Quality of Life

1. **Satisfaction of Sociocultural Life**: Many professionals are drawn to countries that offer vibrant, diverse, and inclusive social environments. These societies often provide a better quality of life, robust cultural activities, and a sense of belonging, enhancing overall personal and family well-being.
2. **Peaceful Interpersonal Relations in Work-Life**: Developed nations often have workplace cultures emphasizing respect, collaboration, and work-life balance. These environments reduce stress and improve job satisfaction, making them attractive to professionals seeking a harmonious and productive work-life.

3. **Desire to Know a Foreign Culture**: The opportunity to experience and immerse oneself in a new culture can be a significant motivator. Learning new languages, understanding different customs, and gaining a global perspective appeal to professionals eager to expand their personal and professional horizons.
4. **Freedom from Political Pressures and Unrest**: Many highly skilled individuals seek countries with stable political climates where they can work and live without fear of political persecution, censorship, or civil unrest. These environments offer a sense of security and freedom that allows professionals to thrive personally and professionally (Oğuzkan, 1971, pp. 55–100).
5. **Better Healthcare and Education**: Access to high-quality healthcare and education is attractive. Countries with well-developed public services and schools especially appeal to professionals with families (Dudu & Rojo, 2022, pp. 148).
6. **Safety and Stability**: Political stability, lower crime rates, and overall safety make developed countries appealing to places to live. The promise of a stable and secure living environment is a big draw for emigrants.

Professional Development

1. **Opportunity to Find a Job in the Field of Specialization:** Many tech professionals struggle to secure positions in Türkiye that match their expertise and training. The lack of job opportunities in Türkiye drives professionals to seek employment in countries where their skills are in higher demand and better recognized.
2. **The Abundance of Financial Opportunities and Resources Needed for Work:** Professionals often leave Türkiye for better pay and the resources they need to do their jobs well. Countries with advanced technology offer higher salaries and state-of-the-art tools and facilities.
3. **Research and Development Opportunities**: Access to advanced research facilities, cutting-edge technology, and the chance to work with leading experts attracts professionals in science, technology, and engineering to other countries. Countries that invest heavily in

R&D attract talent looking to contribute to and benefit from innovative projects.

4. **Recognition and Career Advancement**: The potential for professional recognition and career advancement in global companies and prestigious institutions is a strong attractor. Highly skilled professionals are attracted to places where their work is valued and they can achieve important career goals.

Financial Cost of Education in LDCs Versus Developed Countries

Education costs vary significantly between least developed countries (LDCs) and developed countries due to differences in economic resources, infrastructure, and educational policies. In LDCs, limited funds force hard choices between repaying the national debt and investing in health, education, and the environment.

In less developed countries (LDCs), education costs might be lower in absolute terms but are still very high compared to average income levels. Families often must pay for school fees, uniforms, and teaching materials. Additionally, the lack of schools, especially in rural areas, results in extra costs like transportation and lost labor time, as children could otherwise help with household income. The quality of education is usually lower because of inadequate funding, lack of teaching materials, and poorly trained teachers (UNCTAD, 2023).

In contrast, developed countries invest more in education, leading to higher spending per student. This results in better infrastructure, higher-quality teaching, and more educational resources. Although education can be expensive in these countries, financial aid, scholarships, and student loans help reduce costs. Public education systems often provide free or low-cost education at the primary and secondary levels, reducing the financial burden on families (Wheatley, 2024, pp. 1).

Overall, although education in LDCs might cost less in absolute terms, it is often more expensive relative to income levels and indirect costs. This highlights the need for increased investment and international support to improve educational access and quality in LDCs (UNCTAD, 2023).

Financial Cost of Educating Engineers and Technicians in Türkiye

To estimate the total cost of educating engineers and technicians in Türkiye, we need to add the costs of primary, secondary, and undergraduate education.

Education Stages and Costs according to the TÜİK study (2023).

1. *Primary and Secondary Education*
   (a) **Duration**: 12 years (primary and secondary education)
   (b) **Annual Cost per Student**:
      i. Primary school: $1626
      ii. Secondary school: $1708
      iii. High school: 1873
      iv. Vocational and technical high school: $2586
   (c) Primary and secondary education costs $20,828 for regular high school education and $23,680 for vocational and technical high school education.
2. *Undergraduate Education*
   (a) **Duration**: 4 years for engineers and 2 years for technicians
   (b) **Annual Cost per Student**: Approximately $3561 per year (tuition fees, books, expenses for public universities in Türkiye) and total cost of $14,244 for engineers, and $4024 per year and total cost of $8048 for vocational higher education.

Engineers and Technicians (four years of undergraduate education)

- **Primary and secondary education**: $20,828
- **Undergraduate education (four years)**: $14,244
- **Total cost per student**: $35,072

Technicians (four years of undergraduate education)

- **Primary and secondary education**: $23,680
- **Undergraduate education (two years)**: $8048
- **Total cost per student**: $31,728

Total Financial Cost

To estimate the total financial cost of professionals in these fields who will likely leave Türkiye, we must multiply the cost per student by the number of students trained in each field annually. Approximately 800,000 students graduate from Turkish universities yearly and about 2% move abroad (YÖK, 2025). According to TÜİK (2024), 4.4% of these emigrating graduates are engineers, amounting to around 704 individuals annually. Assuming that some engineers who graduated in previous years also choose to leave, a rough estimate would suggest that approximately 1000 engineers with undergraduate degrees and 500 technicians emigrate from Türkiye each year to work for companies abroad.

The total annual cost of education for engineers who emigrate from Türkiye.

- **Total cost per engineer**: $35,072
- **Number of engineers**: 1000
- **Total annual cost**: $35,072* 1000 = $35,072,000
  The total annual cost of education for technicians who emigrate from Türkiye.
- **Total cost per technician**: $31,528
- **Number of technicians**: 500
- **Total annual cost**: $31,528* 500 = $15,764,000

The total annual cost of education for engineers and technicians who emigrate from Türkiye is about $50,836,000 per year.

Comparison with Educational Costs in Other LDCs

In Türkiye, education costs vary significantly between public and private institutions. Public education for primary and secondary levels is free, although families must still cover uniforms, books, and supplies costs. On the other hand, private schools charge tuition fees ranging from moderate to quite expensive, depending on the school's reputation and location. Higher education in Türkiye also involves tuition fees at both public and private universities. Still, public university fees are generally lower, and scholarships and financial aid options are available to help students manage these costs. Additional expenses such as tutoring, extracurricular activities, and transportation add to the overall cost of education for families.

In contrast, least developed countries (LDCs) often struggle with more significant financial barriers to education. While some LDCs offer free primary education, there are usually still fees for uniforms, books, and supplies. Secondary education typically incurs higher fees, making it less accessible to many families. Private schools in LDCs, which often offer better facilities and teaching standards, are usually out of reach for most families due to their high costs. Higher education is particularly challenging, with limited availability and high expenses, coupled with a scarcity of scholarships and financial aid, making it difficult for students to pursue tertiary education.

The critical differences between Türkiye and LDCs regarding educational costs lie in accessibility, quality, and financial burden. Public education in Türkiye is more accessible and better funded than in LDCs, where even primary education can come with significant costs. The quality of education in Türkiye, both in public and private institutions, is generally higher, providing better learning environments and resources. The financial burden on families in Türkiye is typically lower, thanks to better government support and more available financial aid options. In LDCs, families often face a heavy financial burden due to high costs and a lack of support, which can severely limit educational opportunities for children. In many LDCs, governments usually don't have the money or the motivation to provide proper education. Because of this, some poor parents in these countries have taken it upon themselves to pay for their children's primary education. While school fees are an enormous financial strain for many parents, they prefer to pay these costs rather than have their children go without schooling (Jenkner & Hillman, 2004, pp. 2).

While Türkiye and LDCs face challenges related to the cost of education, Türkiye benefits from a more developed educational infrastructure and comprehensive support mechanisms. This makes education more accessible and affordable for Turkish citizens, whereas families in LDCs struggle with the high costs and limited availability of quality education.

However, the cost of educating highly skilled professionals in Türkiye is much higher than in other least developed countries (LDCs). This is because of Türkiye's significant investment in its people. Understanding this is important because emigration affects Türkiye's economy.

Economic Impact on Türkiye

The emigration of highly skilled professionals from Türkiye, mainly engineers and technicians, has significant adverse economic effects. These impacts include reduced innovation, lower productivity, changes in the labor market, and slower long-term economic growth.

1. **Loss of Human Capital:** The emigration of highly skilled professionals, like engineers and technicians, has caused a significant loss of talent in Türkiye, hurting the country's economy. This brain drain slows down new ideas and lowers productivity, making it hard for the economy to grow and compete. Engineers and technicians are crucial for research and development, which drives technological progress. When they leave, it slows innovation and affects overall economic performance (Dudu & Rojo, 2022).

   When these highly skilled workers leave, it creates problems in the job market, especially in high-tech and specialized areas. Businesses struggle to find qualified people, leading to higher costs and difficulties developing important industries like manufacturing and information technology. This shortage also makes it harder for Türkiye to attract foreign investments and compete globally, weakening its position in the international market (Tuncel, 2021).
2. **Reduced Productivity and Economic Growth:** Highly skilled professionals are essential for increasing economic productivity. When they leave, it lowers overall productivity and affects economic growth. Sectors like technology, engineering, and advanced manufacturing, which depend heavily on specialized skills, are significantly impacted. This reduction in productivity can lead to slower GDP growth and a diminished capacity to develop high-value-added industries (Kirişçi, 2007).
3. **Fiscal Impact:** The fiscal impacts of human capital loss are significant. The Turkish government invests heavily in education and training for these professionals, but when they emigrate, these investments do not yield returns within the country. Additionally, the reduction in tax revenue from high-earning professionals strains public finances, limiting funds available for public services and infrastructure development (Wheatley, 2024, pp. 5).

4. **Labor Market Dynamics:** The departure of highly skilled workers exacerbates labor shortages in critical sectors, leading to increased costs for businesses that need to hire expatriate experts or outsource tasks. The labor shortages can also increase wages for the remaining highly skilled workers, increasing company operational costs. Over time, these dynamics can make Türkiye less attractive for foreign direct investment, further hindering economic development.
5. **Innovation and Entrepreneurship:** Highly skilled professionals are often at the forefront of entrepreneurial activities, establishing startups and driving innovation. Their absence can stifle the entrepreneurial ecosystem, leading to fewer startups, reduced innovation, and a less dynamic economy. This impacts job creation and economic diversification, making the economy more vulnerable to external shocks.
6. **Global Competitiveness:** A continuous outflow of highly skilled professionals weakens Türkiye's position in the global economy. The country's ability to attract and retain international businesses and talent is reduced, making it less competitive. Countries that attract these highly skilled professionals gain an advantage, widening the gap between Türkiye and more advanced economies.
7. **Potential Benefits Through Diaspora Engagement:** While highly skilled professionals leaving Türkiye have many negative impacts, there are potential benefits from connecting with Turks living abroad. These professionals can help by sending money, investing, and sharing knowledge. Programs that encourage working together with these people can reduce some negative impacts and use their skills to help the country grow.

When highly skilled professionals leave Türkiye, it causes problems like less innovation, lower productivity, financial losses, job market issues, and weaker global competitiveness. To fix these problems, the government must create better job opportunities, support innovation, and use the benefits of Turks living abroad. Improving working conditions, offering better career prospects, and ensuring competitive salaries can help keep highly skilled professionals in the country. Policy changes to address why people leave can create a more stable and attractive environment. Additionally, engaging with the Turkish diaspora for knowledge sharing, investments, and collaborations can help reduce some adverse effects of brain drain.

Sector-Specific Impacts, Particularly in Engineering, Technology, and AI

In engineering, the loss of talent leads to project delays and increased costs, as major infrastructure and industrial projects rely heavily on highly skilled engineers for planning, design, and implementation. This affects sectors such as construction, automotive, and energy, where technical expertise is crucial. Additionally, engineers play a vital role in innovation and the development of new technologies; their departure slows down R&D activities, impacting the overall industrial growth and technological advancement of the country.

In the technology sector, including IT and software development, the emigration of highly skilled professionals creates a talent shortage that can limit the tech industry's growth. Companies struggle to fill critical positions, reducing productivity and innovation, making it difficult for Türkiye to attract and retain tech startups and international investments in the tech sector. This talent gap limits the development of high-tech products and services essential for maintaining a competitive edge in the increasingly digital global economy.

The overall impact of highly skilled workers leaving these sectors is decreased economic growth. The country's productivity and economic performance suffer because there are fewer people to innovate and develop new technologies. Additionally, brain drain makes Türkiye less attractive for foreign investments, especially in high-tech industries, because investors prefer countries with a stable and highly skilled workforce to support advanced technologies.

To address this challenge, targeted strategies are needed to keep talent in the country, improve working conditions, and create an environment that supports innovation and growth.

Long-Term Consequences for Innovation and Development

The emigration of highly skilled professionals from Türkiye, especially in engineering, technology, and AI, poses serious challenges to the country's innovation and development. This brain drain can slow research and development (R&D) activities, crucial for technological progress and industrial growth.

One of the most significant long-term impacts is the reduction in Türkiye's innovation ability. Highly skilled professionals in engineering and technology are essential for driving R&D. When they leave, fewer new projects and technological advancements make it harder for Türkiye to compete globally in high-tech industries. This lack of innovation can slow down essential sectors like manufacturing, energy, and information technology, which are vital for economic growth (Wheatley, 2024, pp. 1).

The ongoing loss of highly skilled professionals weakens the country's overall productivity and economic performance. These professionals help develop new products, services, and processes that drive economic growth. Without their contributions, Türkiye may experience slower economic growth, reduced competitiveness, and less ability to attract foreign investments. This economic slowdown can lead to higher unemployment rates and fewer job opportunities for those who remain (Tuncel, 2021).

In the long term, Türkiye's global competitiveness in the technology and engineering sectors is expected to decline. Countries that attract and retain highly skilled professionals will rapidly advance in developing new technologies and industries. As Türkiye loses its talent pool, it may fall behind in adopting and innovating cutting-edge technologies, making it less attractive to international businesses and investors. This can decrease the country's influence and standing in the global market.

The emigration of highly skilled professionals can also expose structural weaknesses within Türkiye's education and professional systems. If the trend of highly skilled professionals leaving Türkiye continues, there may not be enough local talent to fill critical jobs. This could mean relying on foreign experts or outsourcing, which can be expensive and less effective. This dependency can create risks, especially in sectors vital to national security and economic stability.

Persistent brain drain can create a cycle that is hard to break. As more highly skilled professionals leave, those who stay may find it less rewarding to work and live in Türkiye, causing even more people to leave. This ongoing loss of talent can take decades to fix, even with significant efforts and investments in education and training.

Policy Recommendations

Strategies for Retaining Highly Skilled Professionals in Türkiye

To keep highly skilled professionals in Türkiye, well-rounded and detailed policy strategies are needed. These strategies should focus on the economic, social, and professional reasons why people leave the country.

1. **Improve Working Conditions and Compensation: To match international standards,** improving salaries and benefits is essential. This includes offering performance-based incentives, comprehensive healthcare benefits, and retirement plans. Improving workplace conditions and ensuring a healthy work-life balance can make domestic opportunities more attractive.
2. **Invest in Research and Development:** Increased funding for R&D can provide highly skilled professionals with opportunities to engage in cutting-edge projects within Türkiye. Establishing and supporting research institutions, innovation hubs, and technology parks can create an environment that fosters innovation and attracts talent.
3. **Enhance Educational Opportunities:** Investing in higher education and professional development is essential. Scholarships, grants, and funding for advanced degrees and continuous education can help retain talent. Collaborations between universities and industry can provide students with practical experience and job placements upon graduation (OECD, 2023).
4. **Foster a Supportive Environment for Startups and Entrepreneurs:** Creating a supportive startup ecosystem can retain entrepreneurial talent. This includes offering financial incentives, such as tax breaks, grants, and low-interest loans, and providing resources like incubators, mentorship programs, and networking opportunities.
5. **Strengthen Professional Networks and Communities:** Building strong professional networks and communities can enhance job satisfaction and career development. Professional associations, conferences, and networking events can provide platforms for knowledge exchange, collaboration, and career advancement (OECD, 2023).
6. **Promote Quality of Life Enhancements:** Improving the overall quality of life, including healthcare, education, and public services, can make Türkiye a more attractive place to live and work. Investments in infrastructure, public safety, and environmental quality contribute to a higher standard of living, which can retain highly skilled professionals.
7. **Develop Diaspora Engagement Programs:** Working with Turkish professionals living abroad can make use of their skills, knowledge, and connections. Programs that encourage collaboration, investment, and knowledge sharing between these professionals and those

in Türkiye can create more opportunities and reduce the desire to emigrate.

8. **Implement Policy Reforms:** Ensuring political and economic stability is vital. The government needs to be open and honest, reduce unnecessary rules, and make changes that help the economy grow. These steps can create a good environment that makes highly skilled professionals want to stay. Stable politics and fair laws are crucial for gaining their trust.
9. **Offer Recognition and Career Advancement**: Creating clear paths for career growth and recognizing achievements can make jobs more satisfying. Programs that offer awards, promotions, and chances for professional development can encourage highly skilled professionals to stay.

Incentives for Return Migration and Reintegration

Türkiye can use different incentives and supportive policies to encourage highly skilled professionals to return and settle into the country. Financial incentives such as relocation grants, bonuses, and tax breaks can make the transition back home smoother and more appealing. These supports can cover moving expenses, provide settlement allowances, and offer tax relief for a specific time to reduce the financial burden on returnees.

Professional opportunities are also crucial. Job placement programs and special grants in academic and research institutions can attract scholars and researchers back to Türkiye. These opportunities can help them integrate into the local workforce and contribute to innovation and development. By providing clear paths for career growth and recognizing professional achievements, Türkiye can enhance job satisfaction and retain highly skilled professionals.

Support for entrepreneurship is another critical area. Establishing startup incubators, providing low-interest loans and grants, and offering business development services such as market research and financial planning can encourage returnee entrepreneurs to develop businesses in Türkiye. These measures can help them learn about the local market, reduce the risks of starting a new business, and enhance their chances of success.

Furthermore, fostering professional networks and associations and organizing cultural and social programs can help returnees build connections and reintegrate into the local professional and social communities. By implementing these strategies, Türkiye can create a welcoming environment for highly skilled professionals to return and contribute to the country's growth and development.

Improving housing and infrastructure is also vital. Providing affordable housing options, housing grants, and investing in infrastructure, healthcare, and education can enhance the overall quality of life, making Türkiye a more attractive place to live. Streamlining administrative processes related to return migration, such as residency permits and recognition of qualifications, can further facilitate a smoother transition. Clear and comprehensive reintegration policies that outline the available support can make the process more transparent and accessible.

Engaging with the Turkish diaspora through networks and platforms that encourage collaboration and investment in Türkiye can create a supportive environment for returnees. Information campaigns highlighting the opportunities and support available in Türkiye can attract highly skilled professionals back to the country. By implementing these incentives and support mechanisms, Türkiye can create a conducive environment for the return and reintegration of qualified professionals, fostering economic growth and development.

International Cooperation and Policy Alignment to Manage Highly Skilled Migration

International cooperation and policy alignment are essential to effectively manage highly skilled migration and ensure that both sending and receiving countries benefit. This approach requires collaboration in labor market needs, educational systems, and migration policies.

Bilateral and multilateral agreements can provide frameworks for managing highly skilled migration. These agreements can include provisions for mutual recognition of qualifications, making it easier for qualified professionals to move between countries. For example, the European Union's Blue Card initiative aims to attract highly skilled workers from non-EU countries by offering streamlined immigration procedures and better working conditions.

International cooperation in education and training can help align skills with labor market needs. Partnerships between educational institutions in different countries can ensure that curricula are relevant and qualifications are recognized globally. Exchange programs and joint research initiatives can also enhance professionals' skills and prepare them for international job markets.

Policies that allow highly skilled professionals to migrate for a short time can promote knowledge and skill transfer. Programs that let professionals work abroad for a set period before returning home can help build local capacities. These initiatives can be supported by international organizations like the International Organization for Migration (IOM) and the International Labour Organization (ILO), which provide guidelines for ethical recruitment and fair treatment of migrant workers.

Harmonizing immigration policies among countries can reduce barriers to highly skilled migration. Standardizing visa processes, work permits, and residency requirements can make it easier for qualified professionals to move across borders. This can be achieved through regional agreements, like those in the ASEAN Economic Community, which facilitate the movement of highly skilled labor within Southeast Asia.

Encouraging return migration through international cooperation can help reduce the negative impacts of brain drain. Policies incentivizing professionals to return to their home countries after gaining experience abroad can boost local capacities. Financial incentives, job placement programs, and support for entrepreneurship can make returning home more attractive. International organizations can support these efforts by funding and technical assistance for reintegration programs.

Sharing data and conducting joint research on migration trends can help countries develop better policies. By working together to collect and analyze migration data, countries can understand how highly skilled professionals move and how it impacts home and host countries. This information can help make smarter policy decisions and maximize benefits while addressing challenges.

International cooperation can also ensure the migration process is fair and transparent. Organizations like the IOM and ILO promote ethical recruitment standards that protect migrant workers and prevent exploitation. Following these standards can build trust and cooperation between countries involved in highly skilled migration.

Effectively managing highly skilled migration requires strong international cooperation and aligned policies. By creating agreements between countries, forming education and training partnerships, promoting knowledge and skill transfer, standardizing immigration policies, supporting return migration, sharing data, and promoting fair recruitment practices, countries can ensure highly skilled migration benefits both the sending and receiving nations.

Conclusion

Many factors influence why highly skilled professionals leave Türkiye. Economic instability, political unrest, and quality of life concerns push them to leave. Better job opportunities, higher living standards, and career growth in other countries pull them in. To reduce brain drain and support long-term economic growth in Türkiye, addressing these issues with targeted policies and creating a supportive environment for retaining talent is important.

The long-term effects of highly skilled professionals leaving Türkiye include less innovation, slower economic growth, reduced global competitiveness, and potential weaknesses in essential sectors. To tackle these challenges, comprehensive strategies are needed to retain talent, improve working conditions, support innovation, and leverage the Turkish diaspora for knowledge transfer and investment.

The emigration of highly skilled professionals from Türkiye has significant implications for policymakers and stakeholders. A multifaceted approach involving strategic policy interventions and stakeholder engagement is crucial to mitigate the negative impacts and harness potential benefits.

Policymakers must create an environment that offers competitive salaries, career advancement opportunities, and professional development for highly skilled workers. Improving working conditions and providing incentives such as tax breaks, housing subsidies, and relocation grants can help retain talent within the country. By implementing these strategies, Türkiye can create an environment that keeps highly skilled professionals, fostering innovation, economic growth, and overall national development.

Investing in education and continuous professional development is essential. Policymakers should ensure that educational institutions are adequately funded and that curricula are aligned with industry needs. Scholarships, grants, and partnerships with international universities can improve education and training (Dudu & Rojo, 2022).

Creating a supportive environment for startups and innovation can help attract and keep highly skilled professionals. Policies that provide access to funding, mentorship programs, and business incubators can encourage entrepreneurship. Additionally, simplifying regulations and reducing bureaucratic barriers can create a more dynamic business environment (Mahia et al., 2020).

Businesses and industry associations should work with the government to address labor shortages. This can include targeted recruitment drives, vocational training programs, and partnerships with educational institutions to ensure a steady supply of highly skilled professionals.

Policymakers should consider agreements between countries that make it easier for highly skilled professionals to move and share knowledge. Programs that allow temporary migration and knowledge transfer can benefit Türkiye and partner countries. International collaborations in research and development can also attract foreign talent and investments. Connecting with Turkish professionals living abroad can provide significant benefits. Policymakers should create programs to encourage these professionals to invest in Türkiye, share their knowledge, and work on projects together. Platforms that help with networking and collaboration between the diaspora and professionals in Türkiye can enhance these efforts.

Creating favorable conditions for highly skilled professionals to return can help reduce brain drain. Financial incentives, job placement assistance, and support for returning entrepreneurs can encourage qualified professionals to return to Türkiye. Simplifying administrative processes and recognizing international qualifications can make their transition easier.

Improving healthcare, education, and public services can make Türkiye attractive to highly skilled professionals and their families. Investing in infrastructure, safety, and social services is essential to retain talent and improve the overall standard of living.

Ensuring political stability and having good economic policies are crucial for keeping highly skilled professionals in Türkiye. Clear and consistent policies supporting economic growth, transparency, and good governance can build confidence and reduce why people leave.

The emigration of highly skilled professionals from Türkiye presents significant challenges and opportunities. To reduce the negative impacts of brain drain and improve economic and social development, Türkiye should implement strategic policy reforms, foster innovation and entrepreneurship, engage with the diaspora, and enhance the quality of life. Achieving these goals requires collaboration between the government, businesses, educational institutions, and international partners.

References

Akın, M. Ş., & Karadaş, E. (2023). Reasons behind the migration of highly qualified employees from Türkiye: The case of software developers and engineers. *Journal of Economy Culture and Society, 68*, 97–110.

Aydın, Y. (2012). Emigration of highly qualified Turks. In S. Paçaci Elitok & T. Straubhaar (Eds.), *Turkey, migration and the EU: Potentials, challenges and opportunities* (pp. 199–227). Hamburg University Press.

Cazzaniga, M., Jaumotte, M. F., Li, L., Melina, M. G., Panton, A. J., Pizzinelli, C., et al. (2024). *Gen-ai: Artificial intelligence and the future of work.* International Monetary Fund.

Dedeoğlu, D., & Genç, H. D. (2017). Turkish migration to Europe: A modified gravity model analysis. *IZA Journal of Development and Migration, 7*, 1–1.

Dudu, S., & Rojo, T. (2022). The European Union as a destination of Turkish migrants in 2008–2018. *New Perspectives on Turkey, 66*, 140–159.

Elveren, A. Y. (2018). The transformation of regime and gender inequality in Turkey. In *Brain drain and gender inequality in Turkey.* Palgrave Pivot. https://doi.org/10.1007/978-3-319-90860-1_5

Eurostat. (2024). ICT specialists in employment. Retrieved July 4, 2024, from https://ec.europa.eu/eurostat/statistics-explained/index.php?title=ICT_specialists_in_employment

Gürak, H. (1990, 16 Nisan). Türkiye, Beyin Göçünü Önleyerek Söz Sahibi Olur. Gölge Adam Gazetesi, s. 10.

Gürak, H. (2008). Küreselleşme. Retrieved June 28, 2025, from https://www.academia.edu/29706776/K%C3%9CRESELLE%C5%9EME_Prof_Dr_Ay%C5%9Fe_%C4%B0rmi%C5%9Fin_katk%C4%B1lar%C4%B1yla

Gürak, H. (2024). Plundering the skilled workforce. *World Review of Political Economy, 15*(3), 406–421. Retrieved June 28, 2025, from https://www.jstor.org/stable/48812984

Hardan, M. (2024). How Syrian refugees contributed to Turkish economy. *Al-Monitor.* Retrieved July 7, 2024, from https://www.al-monitor.com/originals/2021/05/how-syrian-refugees-contributed-turkish-economy

Jenkner, M. E., & Hillman, M. A. L. (2004). *Educating children in poor countries.* International Monetary Fund. Retrieved July 19, 2024, from https://www.imf.org/external/pubs/ft/issues/issues33/

Kirişci, K. (2007). Turkey: A Country of Transition from Emigration to Immigration. *Mediterranean Politics, 12*(1), 91–97. https://doi.org/10.1080/13629390601136871

Kuşçu, Z. (1979). *Yurt Dışına Beyin Göçü.* T.C. Başbakanlık, Devlet Planlama Teşkilatı Müsteşarlığı, Sosyal Planlama Dairesi. Ankara.

Mahia, R., de Arce, R., Koç, A. A., & Bölük, G. (2020). The short and long-term impact of Syrian refugees on the Turkish economy: A simulation approach.

Turkish Studies, *21*(5), 661–683. Retrieved July 7, 2024, from https://www.tandfonline.com/doi/epdf/10.1080/14683849.2019.1691920?needAccess=true
Marzook, M., Jayawardana, T., & Weerasinghe, R. (2023). Understanding the phenomenon of brain drain: An in-depth analysis of the emigration patterns and implications for IT Professionals in Sri Lanka.
OECD (2023), *Education at a glance 2023: OECD Indicators*. OECD Publishing. https://doi.org/10.1787/e13bef63-en.
Oğuzkan, T. (1971). *Yurt dışında çalışan doktoralı Türkler. Türkiye'den Başka Ülkelere Yüksek Seviyede Eleman Göçü Üzerine Bir Araştırma*. Orta Doğu Teknik Üniversitesi Fen ve Edebiyat Fakültesi Yayınları, Yayın No. 25, Ankara.
Savunma Sanayii Dergilik. (2022). Türkiye'de Beyin Göçü,. Retrieved November 28, 2022, from https://savunmasanayiidergilik.com/tr/HaberDergilik/Turkiye-de-beyin-gocu
Tuncel, K. (2021). Turkey's new emigration wave and its implications. *MANARA Magazine*.
Türkiye Istatistik Kurumu (TÜİK). (2023). Eğitim Harcamaları Istatistikleri, 2023. Retrieved June 28, 2025, from https://data.tuik.gov.tr/Bulten/Index?p=Egitim-Harcamalari-Istatistikleri-2023-53557
Türkiye Istatistik Kurumu (TÜİK). (2024). *Göç Istatistikleri*. Available at: TÜİK Göç İstatistikleri. Retrieved June 28, 2025, from https://data.tuik.gov.tr/Bulten/Index?p=Uluslararasi-Goc-Istatistikleri-2024-54083&dil=1
UNCTAD. 2023. *Least Developed Countries Report 2023*. Retrieved July 7, 2024, from https://unctad.org/system/files/official-document/ldc2023_en.pdf
UNDESA (United Nations Department of Economic and Social Affairs). (2017). International migrant stock: The 2017 revision. Retrieved July 18, 2024, from https://www.un.org/development/desa/pd/content/international-migrant-stock
Wheatley, M. C. (2024). Navigating the digital divide: A global perspective. *Premier Journal of Computer Science*, *1*, 100003. Retrieved July 7, 2025, from https://premierscience.com/wp-content/uploads/2024/11/pjcs-24-356-.pdf
World Bank. (2011). Global bilateral migration. Retrieved July 5, 2019, from https://databank.worldbank.org/source/global-bilateral-migration
World Bank. (2017). Migration and remittances data. Retrieved July 18, 2024, from https://www.worldbank.org/en/topic/migrationremittancesdiasporaissues/brief/migration-remittances-data
World Bank. (2025). Türkiye. Overview. Retrieved July 6, 2025, from https://www.worldbank.org/en/country/turkey/overview?
YÖK. (2025). Yükseköğretim Bilgi Sistemi. Retrieved June 29, 2025, from https://istatistik.yok.gov.tr/

CHAPTER 5

Brain Drain in the Digital Age: A Qualitative Analysis of Turkish IT and AI Professionals' Migration Decisions

Haşmet Gökirmak and Fuat Sekmen

Introduction

The Turkish technology sector is expanding by investing in digital infrastructure, techno parks, and government incentives to keep up with technological development in the world. One of the main challenges to the industry is to educate and train in artificial intelligence (AI), software development, and information technology (IT) fields. Yet another critical problem is that these highly skilled professionals find better opportunities elsewhere in the world. The reasons for professionals leaving the country

H. Gökirmak (✉)
Department of Business and Management Sciences, Istanbul Sabahattin Zaim University, İstanbul, Turkey
e-mail: hasmet.gokirmak@izu.edu.tr

F. Sekmen
Faculty of Political Science-Department of Economics, Sakarya University, Sakarya, Turkey
e-mail: sekmen@sakarya.edu.tr

H. Gürak (ed.), *The Economics of Migration of Highly Skilled Workers from Türkiye*,
https://doi.org/10.1007/978-3-032-10606-3_5

include economic instability, limited research funding, low private-sector wages, and restricted opportunities for professional advancement. Highly skilled professionals in information and communication technologies have the highest emigration rates (6.8%), followed by those in the engineering and natural sciences disciplines. Molecular biology and genetics, biomedical engineering, and computer engineering graduates are among the highest non-return rates (TÜİK). In addition to physical emigration, many professionals work remotely for foreign firms, creating a "virtual brain drain." The physical and virtual brain drain requires a deeper investigation into personal and structural drivers causing the emigration of highly skilled professionals from the Turkish tech ecosystem.

The Turkish Statistical Institute (TÜİK, 2024) *statistics show that* in 2024, the brain drain rate among higher education graduates in Türkiye reached 2%. The first choice for these graduates is to move to the USA. According to TÜİK, the brain drain rate for higher education graduates was 1.6% in 2015, increasing to 2% by 2023. The rate for women stands at 1.6%, while for men, it is 2.4% for 2023.

TÜİK data show that the highest brain drain rates are among science and technology-related graduates. The graduates from Information and Communication Technologies (ICT) programs demonstrate the highest emigration rate at 6.8%, followed by those in Engineering, Manufacturing, and Construction at 4.4%, and Natural Sciences, Mathematics, and Statistics at 2.6%.

The highest among bachelor's degree programs are Molecular Biology and Genetics graduates with the highest brain drain rate at 17.9%, followed by Biomedical Engineering (10.2%), Industrial Engineering (9.8%), Electronic Engineering (9.1%), Mathematics Engineering (8.9%), and Computer Engineering (8.4%). These statistics suggest a concentration of emigration among highly trained individuals in Türkiye's most innovation-intensive academic fields. This outflow of highly skilled professionals limits the country's technological innovation capacity.

Bachelor's degree holders prefer the USA the most, with 21.4%, followed by Germany at 17.5%, the UK at 11.2%, the Netherlands at 6.9%, and Canada at 4.9%. Business graduates mostly move to the USA and Canada, while computer engineering graduates predominantly choose the UK and the Netherlands. The Council of Higher Education (YÖK) reported that between 2008 and 2017, 2,442,039 individuals graduated with a bachelor's degree from universities in Türkiye. With a 2% brain drain rate, this equates to 48,841 individuals. YOK statistics also show that

47,602 university graduates left Türkiye between 2007 and 2016 (YÖK, 2025).

Brain drain is also a broader trend across Eastern Europe, the Middle East, North Africa (MENA), and Türkiye. Easier access to Western European countries and the U.S. challenges retaining highly skilled professionals, particularly in science, technology, engineering, and mathematics (STEM) fields. Eastern Europe lost many highly skilled workers once they joined the European Union (EU). EU accession facilitated labor mobility and intensified the outflow of educated youth and tech workers to Western Europe. More favorable salaries and research opportunities are often the reason for this outflow. The MENA region, however, has been experiencing political instability, underinvestment in research and development, and limited institutional autonomy, leading to sustained emigration of skilled professionals. In both cases, brain drain has raised concerns about the long-term potential for technological advancement and economic diversification for the host countries (Fakih & El Baba, 2023, pp. 19). Türkiye's situation is similar but is further complicated by its unique geopolitical position and being both a sender and, at times, a transit country for skilled migration.

The primary objective of this chapter is to explore the motivations, experiences, and leading factors that drive the emigration of artificial intelligence (AI) and information technology (IT) professionals. The research uses a qualitative approach to understand how and why these leave Türkiye to pursue career opportunities abroad. Specifically, the study investigates personal aspirations, professional constraints, and broader socioeconomic factors. Political dynamics that influence skilled migration are also examined. Hence, this study aims to contribute to the literature on brain drain by providing narrative-based insights that complement macro-level data and offer implications for policy, workforce development, and talent retention strategies for Türkiye's technology sector.

Theoretical Framework

The AI and IT professionals emigrate from Türkiye due to several factors ranging from individual preferences to broader structural factors. Although the economic motives are often highlighted, emigration decisions are usually based on multiple causes. These decisions reflect a complex interaction of personal aspirations, perceived opportunities, institutional environments, and systemic constraints. Four key theoretical perspectives explain the emigration of highly skilled professionals. The Push-Pull Model of Migration identifies contextual drivers and attractions. The Human Capital Theory views migration as an investment in skills and future returns. The Expectancy-Value Theory (EVT) focuses on motivational and identity-related dimensions of career decision-making. The Institutional Theory places migration within the quality and legitimacy of state and organizational institutions. These theories offer a comprehensive view of why highly skilled professionals leave Türkiye for better professional opportunities abroad.

The brain drain has been extensively studied within the broader context of skilled migration, with several theoretical frameworks to explain its causes and consequences. The most widely used model is **the push-pull framework**, explaining migration due to unfavorable conditions in the country of origin (push factors) and attractive opportunities in destination countries (pull factors). In Türkiye's tech sector, push factors may include limited career advancement, economic instability, or political uncertainty. At the same time, pull factors often include higher salaries, better research opportunities, and improved quality of life abroad.

Human Capital Theory explores the individual decision-making process causing skilled migration. In this theory, migration is viewed as an investment decision in which individuals try to maximize returns on their education and skills by relocating to countries offering greater rewards for their qualifications. The emigration of AI and IT professionals from Türkiye reflects rational responses to global labor market conditions. These frameworks provide a valuable foundation for interpreting the complex motivations behind high-skill emigration and offer a viewpoint for analyzing the interview data collected in this study.

Expectancy-Value Theory (EVT) is a psychological framework that explains motivation and decision-making, including career choices, by focusing on two core factors: expectancy and value. This theory suggests that individuals are more likely to pursue a particular goal or task (such as a career path) when they (1) expect to succeed in it and (2) value the outcome of that success.

EVT helps explain why people choose specific fields of study. For example, a student might decide to become an engineer not only because they believe they are good at math and science but also because they enjoy problem-solving, see engineering as a prestigious identity, and believe it offers stable job prospects. Conversely, they may avoid a different path if the cost is perceived as too high, such as long years of schooling or financial risk.

EVT is particularly useful in understanding gender, socioeconomic, and cultural differences in career choices, as social context, stereotypes, and access to opportunities shape expectations and values. It offers an alternative to purely economic theories by integrating subjective perceptions and motivations into career development and educational attainment models.

Institutional Theory explains how institutions, defined as the formal rules, informal norms, and organizational structures that shape behavior, affect decision-making, behavior, and outcomes in organizations and states. Institutional Theory emphasizes how institutions influence what individuals *can*, *should*, and *will* do, often beyond rational calculation or economic incentives.

Institutional Theory helps explain emigration from Türkiye by shifting the focus from individual-level motivations to the role of institutional environments—within the state and organizations—in shaping migration decisions. Rather than viewing migration solely as a response to wages or job opportunities (as in Human Capital Theory), Institutional Theory highlights how weak, rigid, or delegitimized institutions can erode individuals' trust in the system, driving them to seek alternatives abroad.

Literature Review

Mary Christine Wheatley's review article "Navigating the Digital Divide: A Global Perspective" (2024) couples contemporary scholarship and statistics to show that the digital divide is no longer a narrow issue of infrastructure but a multidimensional driver of social inequality. She points out the contrast in internet penetration among nations, exceeding 80% in most high-income countries yet less than 20% in many low- and middle-income countries. She notes the gaps between urban and rural areas as well as among vulnerable populations such as low-income households, the elderly, and persons with disabilities.

Wheatley argues that limited internet connectivity creates educational losses (exacerbated by the COVID-19 pivot to online learning), reduces access to telemedicine, weakens labor market prospects, and lowers levels of civic engagement. Her study covers case studies of South Korea, Estonia, and Rwanda. The review shows that effective public investment and early digital-literacy programs can produce rapid gains in these countries. However, regions in sub-Saharan Africa, rural Asia, and parts of

Latin America remain constrained by high costs, weak policy frameworks, and insufficient skills training.

The article surveys solutions, including targeted infrastructure funds, competitive Internet Service Provider (ISP) regulation, low-cost mobile devices, community networks, NGO-led literacy campaigns, and satellite internet solutions. Wheatley argues that emerging technologies such as 5G, IoT, and blockchain could bridge or further widen the gap, depending on affordability and skills diffusion. The study suggests recommendations, including integrating digital-access targets into national development strategies, embedding digital competencies in education, scaling low-bandwidth tele-health platforms, and leveraging public-private partnerships to finance last-mile connectivity. These suggestions ensure that advances in digital technology translate into inclusive socioeconomic development rather than widening the gaps.

Empirical research on Türkiye's brain drain in STEM and tech sectors has increasingly moved beyond aggregate trends to incorporate register-based evidence and discipline-specific insights. An important contribution by Metin (2023) analyzes administrative data from 63,787 Turkish IT graduates. It reports an 11.4% non-return rate in 2020, based on 7284 individuals who did not return after completing their education in Türkiye. Computer and electrical/electronic engineering were most affected, accounting for approximately 73% of the IT-sector brain drain. Complementing this, Metin (2023) examines broader bachelor's degree graduates (total about 1.73 million) and identifies an overall 3.23% brain drain rate in 2020, noting a substantial gender gap: 3.62% for males versus 2.84% for females, and migration concentrated toward the USA (22.4%), Germany (14%), and the UK (11.6%).

While these studies provide rigorous quantitative benchmarks, qualitative and field-based research remains limited. One emerging topic is the concept of "virtual brain drain," referring to AI and IT professionals who remain resident in Türkiye but engage in remote employment for foreign firms, effectively exporting skills and income without physical relocation. However, in-depth analyses of such professionals' motivations, lived experiences, and decision-making processes are limited.

Historical qualitative studies, such as earlier web-survey investigations of return intentions by Tansel and Güngör (2003), highlight non-financial factors influencing migration decisions (e.g., family ties, social environment, political context) alongside wage differentials. These findings continue to be referenced, but more recent, high-tech sector-specific qualitative studies remain rare.

Beyond Türkiye, broader simulation and modelling efforts—such as Gürsoy and Badur's agent-based model of brain drain dynamics (2021), illuminate the role of socioeconomic forecasts, network effects, and policy barriers in emigration flows. However, they are more abstract and not Türkiye-specific regarding qualitative narrative content. They argue that network effects are important in facilitating one's emigration by increasing the chances of finding employment abroad and providing social support.

The quantitative register-based contributions over the past few years have demonstrated robust brain drain rates, especially among IT graduates. Yet there is a marked gap in qualitative, interpretive research, particularly regarding AI/IT professionals' narratives, decision logics, and experiences as part of Türkiye's tech migration. This study intends to fill that gap through semi-structured interviews and thematic analysis, offering a deeper, more contextualized account to complement the growing body of macro-level research.

Docquier and Rapoport's seminal review paper, "Globalization, Brain Drain and Development" (2012), synthesizes four decades of economic research on high-skilled emigration—commonly termed "brain drain"—within the broader framework of globalization. The authors examine skilled migration's determinants and evolving patterns, assess its developmental consequences for source countries, and consider the corresponding policy implications. They highlight the rapid growth of high-skill migration relative to low-skill migration, noting its increasing prominence as a structural feature of globalization, particularly concerning OECD countries. Major countries of origin for high-skilled migrants include India, China, the Philippines, and Mexico. The primary drivers identified are economic incentives such as wage differentials and employment prospects, educational attainment levels, historical and geographical linkages (e.g., colonial ties and proximity), and network effects stemming from existing diaspora communities. The authors categorize the intellectual evolution of brain drain studies into three distinct waves: the first wave (1960s) interpreted brain drain as either neutral or beneficial due to factors such as remittances and the global public good nature of human capital; the second wave (1970s), led by Bhagwati and others, emphasized the negative externalities for sending countries, including increased inequality and the phenomenon of "brain waste" due to skill mismatches; and the third wave (post-1990s) adopted a more nuanced perspective, integrating endogenous growth models to demonstrate that, under certain conditions, brain drain can generate positive outcomes—so-called beneficial brain drain—through increased education incentives, return migration, and diaspora-driven knowledge and capital flows. The paper identifies five principal channels through which skilled emigration affects sending countries: human capital formation, remittance inflows, return migration, diaspora networks (which facilitate trade, investment, and technology transfer), and fiscal externalities stemming from the loss of public investment in education. Through case studies—including the medical brain drain in Africa, the migration of European scientists to the USA, and the role of Indian IT professionals abroad—the authors illustrate both the sectoral vulnerabilities and potential development gains associated with skilled migration. They argue against restrictive emigration policies, advocating instead for strategies that harness diaspora networks, enhance domestic opportunities for skilled workers, promote return and circular migration, and explore international mechanisms to redistribute the benefits of migration more equitably. The paper argues that brain drain is a complex, context-dependent phenomenon with the capacity to either constrain or catalyze development, depending on the institutional and policy environment of the sending country.

Ismail Öneri's master's thesis, "Brain Drain from Turkey: Causes, Processes, and Consequences" (2019), provides a qualitative investigation into the recent increase in high-skilled emigration from Türkiye, particularly after the 2010s. The study examines the primary causes, decision-making processes, and long-term expectations of Turkish professionals who have chosen to emigrate. He interviewed 12 participants, mostly in their 30s, with graduate degrees and employed in high-skill sectors. His research focuses on those who had migrated to countries such as Germany, the Netherlands, and Canada, or were actively preparing to do so. The findings reveal a multidimensional set of push and pull factors. Push factors include political instability and authoritarianism, particularly in the aftermath of the 2016 coup attempt, constraints on academic freedom and freedom of expression, the weakening of meritocratic systems, economic insecurity, and a sense of exclusion or alienation experienced by certain social groups. Pull factors encompass higher standards of living, greater academic and professional opportunities, stronger political freedoms, and the perception of fairness and transparency in institutions abroad. Migration decisions were often formed progressively, influenced by political events (such as the Gezi Park protests and the failed coup), growing feelings of alienation within Türkiye, peer influence from friends or colleagues abroad, and overseas education, which frequently served as a migration channel. The study also highlights the complex experiences of identity and belonging among emigrants, many of whom reported a simultaneous sense of personal liberation abroad and emotional attachment to Türkiye, coupled with a detachment from the prevailing political and cultural climate. Notably, most participants indicated no intention of returning to Türkiye soon unless significant political and systemic reforms occurred, particularly the restoration of academic and professional freedoms and improved economic conditions. Öneri concludes that economic considerations and deep political and psychological dissatisfaction drive the contemporary wave of brain drain from Türkiye. In this context, emigration becomes a form of silent protest and individual exit from a deteriorating institutional environment. To mitigate long-term human capital losses, the study recommends that Türkiye pursue democratic reforms, strengthen institutional and academic freedoms, restore economic and professional mobility, and adopt inclusive, merit-based governance practices.

Financial Cost of Educating Engineers and Technicians in Türkiye

To estimate the total cost of educating AI and IT specialists in Türkiye, we need to add the costs of primary, secondary, and undergraduate education.

Education Stages and Costs according to the TÜİK study (2023):

1. *Primary and Secondary Education*
   (a) **Duration**: 12 years (primary and secondary education)
   (b) **Annual Cost per Student**:
      i. Primary school: $1626
      ii. Secondary school: $1708
      iii. High school: 1873
      iv. Vocational and technical high school: $2586
   (c) Primary and secondary education costs $20,828 for regular high school education and $23,680 for vocational and technical high school education.

2. *Undergraduate Education*
   (a) **Duration**: 4 years for engineers and 2 years for technicians
   (b) **Annual Cost per Student**: Approximately $3561 per year (tuition fees, books, expenses for public universities in Türkiye) and total cost of $14,244 for AI and IT specialists, and $4024 per year and total cost of $8048 for vocational higher education.

AI and IT Specialists (4 Years of Undergraduate Education)

- **Primary and secondary education**: $20,828
- **Undergraduate education (4 years)**: $14,244
- **Total cost per student**: $35,072

Total Financial Cost

To estimate the total financial cost of professionals in these fields who will likely leave Türkiye, we must multiply the cost per student by the number of students trained in each field annually. Approximately 800,000 students graduate from Turkish universities yearly and about 2% move abroad (YÖK, 2025). According to TÜİK (2024), 6.8% of these emigrating graduates are AI and IT specialists, amounting to around 1088 individuals annually. Assuming that some AI and IT specialists who graduated in previous years also choose to leave, a rough estimate would suggest that approximately 1200 AI and IT specialists with undergraduate degrees and 500 technicians emigrate from Türkiye each year to work for companies abroad.

The total annual cost of education for AI and IT specialists who emigrate from Türkiye.

- **Total cost per engineer**: $35,072
- **Number of engineers**: 1200
- **Total annual cost**: $35,072* 1000 = $42,086,400

Research Gaps

While recent years have witnessed an increase in quantitative analyses of brain drain from Türkiye, drawing on administrative registers, TÜİK statistics (TÜİK, 2024), and OECD migration data (OECD, 2024), there remains a notable scarcity of qualitative, field-based studies that explore the subjective experiences and decision-making processes of emigrating professionals. Most existing research focuses on aggregate trends and demographic patterns, providing valuable macro-level insights but offering limited understanding of the micro-level motivations, aspirations, and emotional landscapes of individuals within the tech sector. Moreover, the unique challenges faced by subgroups—such as early career professionals, women in tech, or remote workers contributing to the so-called virtual brain drain—are often underexamined or treated superficially. Few studies engage with in-depth interviews, narrative analysis, or ethnographic methods that would illuminate the lived realities of Türkiye's AI and IT professionals navigating global labor markets. This study addresses these gaps by offering a grounded, interpretive account of skilled emigration based on first-hand testimony, complementing and enriching the predominantly quantitative literature on Türkiye's tech brain drain.

Methodology

This study uses a qualitative research methodology. The interviews were conducted to explore complex, subjective experiences such as the motivations, objectives, and other factors influencing the emigration decisions of highly skilled professionals. This study aims to generate in-depth insights into individuals' lived experiences and perspectives within Türkiye's technology sector.

Semi-structured in-depth interviews were used as the primary data source. A semi-structured interview is a qualitative research method that combines a pre-determined set of open questions (questions that prompt discussion) with the opportunity for the interviewer to explore themes or responses further. This methodological choice is well-suited for capturing the complex interplay of personal, institutional, and systemic factors in brain drain.

Sample and Data Collection

This study employed purposive and snowball sampling strategies to identify participants with relevant experiences and insights. Purposive sampling was used to ensure the inclusion of individuals who met specific criteria central to the research objectives—namely, Turkish nationals who have professional experience in artificial intelligence (AI) or information technology (IT) and who migrated abroad in recent years. This method allowed for the deliberate selection of participants with the expertise and background necessary to provide rich, contextually grounded data. To expand the sample and reach potentially hard-to-access individuals, snowball sampling was subsequently applied: initial participants were asked to refer peers or colleagues who met the inclusion criteria. This combined approach was instrumental in accessing a geographically dispersed and professionally mobile population while enhancing the diversity and depth of perspectives captured in the study.

Data was collected through semi-structured interviews with nine participants. Appendix 1 presents the questionnaire used for the semi-structured deep interviews.

The data were analyzed using thematic analysis. This analytical approach enabled the identification of both commonalities and divergences in participants' migration experiences and perceptions of Türkiye's tech sector.

Findings

The nine AI/IT professionals in this study share similar characteristics: all hold at least a bachelor's degree in computer-related fields (five master's, three PhDs) and had built early-to-mid-career experience in Türkiye, yet each ultimately left because push forces outweighed local attractions. They describe a decisive "inflation shock" after 2021, in combination with rapid Turkish lira devaluation and rising living costs. Economic instability, political-social disillusionment, nepotism, impaired rule of law, and an ever-present sense of crisis eroded their confidence in Türkiye's future. Professionally, participants felt their skills were recognized but underutilized: cloud-use bans in finance, scarcity of senior mentors, toxic work culture, and long commutes limited innovation and career growth. The predictable, rules-based environments that offered higher real income, better work-life balance, streamlined bureaucracy, and calmer daily life were the attracting factors for them. Several highlighted efficient public services and institutional support networks that eased their adaptation to the host country. While two hope to return eventually and three remain conditionally open, most see little prospect of returning without deep structural changes, specifically macroeconomic stability, an independent judiciary, and meritocratic governance. In essence, their decisions align with Push-Pull, Human-Capital, Expectancy-Value, and Institutional theories: acute economic and political pressures at home, combined with credible expectations of safer, more rewarding careers abroad, drove a collective exit that seems durable unless Türkiye undergoes systemic reform.

Discussion

The interview evidence sits comfortably inside the broad contours of the literature reviewed, yet it also sharpens and extends several strands of that work. First, Mary Christine Wheatley's (2024) global "digital-divide" perspective is only tangentially reflected in the engineers' stories. All nine already enjoy ubiquitous broadband and cloud-based workflows abroad, so connectivity is not a push factor. Instead, participants implicitly contrast Türkiye's regulatory frictions and day-to-day unpredictability with the seamless, rules-based digital environments they now inhabit, suggesting that once basic access is universal, institutional quality—not raw infrastructure—becomes the decisive differentiator.

Turning to Metin's (2023) register-based analysis of Turkish IT graduates, the interviews confirm its headline numbers and destination pattern—most migrants land in the Netherlands, Germany, the USA, or another EU hub and mirror the male-skewed profile. The qualitative data add temporal granularity: eight respondents identify the late-2021 lira collapse as the exact moment hesitancy turned into action, a post-cut-off event that quantitative datasets have yet to capture.

The narratives also resonate with the classic push-pull insights of Tansel and Güngör (2003), reaffirming that political alienation, perceived nepotism, and social polarization matter as much as wages. Yet today, those non-pecuniary pressures interact with an acute macroeconomic shock, making migration feel less like a long-term aspiration and more like an emergency exit.

Gürsoy and Badur's (2021) agent-based model finds support too: six participants cite prior study abroad, expatriate friends, or LinkedIn referrals as critical enablers, validating the predicted network externalities. However, the interviewees introduce a fresh mechanism that the model does not anticipate—the scarcity of senior technical mentors and cloud-use bans in Turkish finance, which blocks skill utilization at home and accelerates departure.

Docquier and Rapoport's (2012) multi-channel framework likewise holds that wage differentials, diaspora ties, and institutional quality appear in the transcripts. Yet the engineers rank legal certainty and meritocracy above pure income growth when contemplating return, suggesting that for mid-career tech workers, institutional trust now eclipses remittances or education incentives as the pivotal factor.

Finally, the interviews strongly echo Ismail Öneri's (2019) qualitative thesis: political authoritarianism, economic insecurity, and a sense of alienation drive exit, while meaningful repatriation seems unlikely without systemic reform. The new data contributes to post-pandemic details—the inflation shock as the tipping point and tech-sector-specific bottlenecks, such as mentor gaps and restrictive cloud regulations—thereby updating and deepening the earlier narrative.

In sum, the testimonies corroborate the quantitative benchmarks and classic theories in your review but enrich them with real-time catalysts and sector-specific frictions, filling the qualitative gap your study set out to address.

Several factors emerged from the nine interviews that add texture to—or fall outside—the patterns documented in the existing literature. First, respondents pinpoint a single macro-event—the late-2021 lira crash—as the moment "abstract worries" became an urgent plan to leave. Whereas prior studies note gradual wage-gap calculations, the engineers describe a sudden, visceral realization that their savings and salaries could halve in days, converting long-term emigration musings into immediate action.

Second, political disappointment is a daily constraint on professional integrity. Participants link "nepotism and immorality" to delayed promotions, arbitrary project choices, and a sense that meritocratic effort is fruitless. Rather than events like the 2016 coup, this personal loss of trust in institutions ultimately undercuts their willingness to invest careers in Türkiye.

Third, the interviews highlighted tech-sector bottlenecks rarely detailed in the literature. Two stand out: (1) *senior-mentor scarcity*—teams lack mid-career technical leaders, leaving ambitious engineers without role models or guidance; and (2) *regulatory cloud bans* in finance and other critical industries that force teams to reinvent mature tools locally, hindering both learning curves and product sophistication.

Fourth, a toxic work-culture triad—long commutes, limited vacation, and 24/7 "crisis mode" management—combines with the startup ecosystem's thin funding and risk aversion to create a capability and well-being mismatch. Even engineers who found their skills *recognized* felt they were *underutilized* or pressed into maintenance work rather than genuine R&D.

Finally, return intentions depend on institutional trust rather than income differentials. Most interviewees say they would reconsider Türkiye only after judicial reform and credible meritocracy are in place. Economic recovery alone, they stress, would not erase memories of sudden rule changes or politically driven career ceilings.

Together, these reasons highlight an interaction of inflation shock, political alienation, skill-deployment barriers, and startup ecosystem weaknesses that is largely absent from aggregate surveys. They suggest that reversing tech-talent outflows will require more than salary incentives or infrastructure upgrades; it will depend on rebuilding predictable, rules-based environments in which advanced skills, mentorship structures, and entrepreneurial risk-taking can all flourish.

Reversing—or at least slowing—the out-migration of Türkiye's AI/IT talent will require action on four tightly linked fronts. The first is restoring macroeconomic and institutional confidence.

Every interviewee located the late-2021 lira collapse and the perceived politicization of hiring and promotion as the decisive push to leave. Credible, forward-looking monetary policy that reins in inflation, plus judicial reforms that make contract enforcement and career advancement visibly merit-based, would remove the single biggest "flight trigger." The OECD's 2024 report likewise stresses that a stable macro framework and predictable courts are preconditions for retaining high-skill workers (OECD, 2024).

The second is unblocking sector-specific capability bottlenecks. Engineers blamed two home-grown frictions rarely covered in the literature: a shortage of senior technical mentors and finance-sector rules that ban mainstream cloud services. Lifting or sandboxing those cloud restrictions, while pairing local teams with experienced diaspora engineers through paid "returning-expert" tracks, would instantly raise the ceiling on what domestic R&D teams can build. TÜBİTAK's new €15 million CoCirculation3 and 2232 "Returning Researchers" calls already provide a funding spine for such programs (TÜBİTAK, 2025).

The third is deepening and de-risking the startup ecosystem. Interviewees described thin venture funding and risk-averse corporates that confine them to maintenance work. Special economic zones offering zero corporate tax for R&D, fast-track stock-option rules, and a government "fund-of-funds" that co-invests alongside Venture Capital (VC) (an idea flagged in a recent TechPulse Türkiye policy brief) would expand the pool of high-impact projects on home soil. A lighter-touch bankruptcy regime—so failure does not equal lifetime black-listing—would further normalize entrepreneurial risk.

The fourth is turning the new "Türkiye Tech Visa" into a two-way bridge. An outward-oriented version of the 2024 Tech Visa, which already lures foreign founders and senior engineers with expedited residency and tax perks, could also serve returnees. Matching it with housing subsidies in tech hubs, automatic spousal work permits, and a 30 % tax-free income ruling (mirroring the Dutch scheme many migrants now enjoy) would tackle the quality-of-life calculus favoring Europe.

Taken together, these four levers—macro stability and rule of law, frictionless tech tooling plus mentorship pipelines, risk-tolerant capital, and globally competitive living-and-tax conditions—directly address the inflation shock, political disillusionment, and startup-ecosystem gaps that the interviewees said pushed them out. Implemented in concert, they offer the most straightforward route to slowing, and eventually reversing, Türkiye's AI/IT brain drain.

Conclusion

This qualitative study of nine emigrated Turkish AI/IT professionals confirms—and sharpens—existing evidence on the country's tech-talent outflow. First, an acute inflation shock in late 2021 turned long-standing emigration musings into immediate action, making macroeconomic volatility the single most powerful push. Second, political disillusionment and perceived nepotism eroded confidence in career-long meritocracy, while day-to-day "crisis mode" work cultures, long commutes, and limited vacation amplified frustration. Third, respondents highlighted sector-specific capability bottlenecks—notably a shortage of senior technical mentors and cloud-service bans in finance—that stalled skill utilization and innovation. Conversely, destination countries offered predictable institutions, higher real incomes, robust R&D tool-chains, and better work-life balance, satisfying professional ambitions and personal well-being. Return intentions remain low: most participants would reconsider only after durable macroeconomic stability, credible judicial independence, and clear merit-based advancement are in place. In sum, reversing Türkiye's AI/IT brain drain will require more than salary incentives or infrastructure upgrades; it hinges on rebuilding a rules-based, high-capability environment where advanced skills, entrepreneurial risk-taking, and everyday life can flourish without perpetual uncertainty.

Study Limitations

This study's insights should be read with several caveats in mind. First, the nine interviewees constitute a small, self-selected sample recruited online, so the voices of professionals who either remained in Türkiye or emigrated but declined participation are absent; their motives or constraints might differ substantially (classic self-selection bias). Second, the group is regionally and sector-skewed: most hold computer-engineering degrees from Istanbul-based universities and now live in Northwestern Europe or North America, leaving Anatolian graduates, women (only one in the sample), and destinations such as the Gulf or East Asia under-represented. Third, timing effects matter: all participants left within the past decade—many after the 2021 lira crash—so their narratives may over-emphasize recent macro-shocks and understate slower-burn drivers that influenced earlier cohorts. Fourth, the data rely on retrospective self-report; recall and rationalization biases could color how turning points are described, while social-desirability pressures may lead respondents to foreground meritocratic ideals over purely financial motives. Fifth, interviews were conducted and analyzed in English, which might have constrained nuance for those whose native language is Turkish, potentially filtering emotional content or culturally specific idioms. Finally, because the study focuses solely on AI/IT professionals, its findings cannot be generalized to other STEM or health sectors without further discipline-specific investigation. These limitations underscore the need for larger, more diverse samples, mixed-methods designs, and longitudinal follow-up to capture the full complexity of Türkiye's high-skill migration dynamics.

Future Research Suggestions

Future inquiry should move beyond a small, self-selected expatriate cohort to capture the full spectrum of Turkish tech-talent flows. A priority is a large-N, mixed-methods panel that tracks three comparison groups—emigrants, "virtual migrants" who export skills remotely, and stayers—over several years; linking survey waves to administrative wage, patent, and tax data would reveal how motives and outcomes diverge across pathways and over time. Second, researchers should oversample under-represented strata—women, Anatolian universities, non-EU destinations, and mid-career returnees—to test whether the inflation-politics-capability narrative holds outside the Istanbul-to-Europe corridor. Third, qualitative work could drill into the sector-specific frictions uncovered here: ethnographic studies inside finance, defense, and startup clusters could verify how cloud-regulation bans, mentor scarcity, or venture-capital thinness play out on engineering shop floors. Fourth, a network-analytic approach that maps LinkedIn and GitHub ties before and after migration would quantify the role of diaspora referrals and knowledge spill-overs suggested anecdotally in these interviews. Finally, policy-experiment evaluations—for example, of Türkiye's Tech-Visa and TÜBİTAK "Returning Researchers" schemes—should be embedded from the outset, combining applicant micro-data with counterfactual matching to see whether improved tool-chains, tax breaks, or judicial reforms genuinely bend brain drain trajectories. Collectively, these designs would temper recall bias, broaden sectoral and geographic coverage, and generate causal leverage on which economic, institutional, or ecosystemic levers most effectively retain or re-attract Türkiye's AI/IT talent.

Appendix

Questionnaire: Emigration of AI and IT Professionals from Türkiye

We are conducting a research study to understand why AI and IT professionals choose to emigrate from Türkiye. Your responses will remain confidential and will be used solely for academic purposes. Please answer the following questions in as much detail as you are comfortable sharing.

Section I: Background Information

1. Full Name (optional):
2. Age:
3. Gender (optional):
4. Current country of residence:
5. Year you moved abroad (if applicable):
6. What is your educational background (degree, field, university)?
7. What area(s) of AI or IT do you work in?
8. Briefly describe your professional background and your last job in Türkiye:

Section II: Emigration Decision

9. What initially made you consider moving abroad?
10. Was there a specific turning point that finalized your decision?
11. Did you consider alternatives within Türkiye before deciding to emigrate? Why or why not?

Section III: Push Factors (Türkiye)

12. What challenges or limitations did you experience as an AI/IT professional in Türkiye?
13. Did you feel your skills and potential were being fully recognized and utilized in Türkiye?
14. To what extent did political, economic, or social conditions in Türkiye influence your decision?
15. Did family or personal considerations influence your decision?

Section IV: Pull Factors (Destination Country)

16. Why did you choose your current country of residence?
17. What aspects of life or work abroad appealed most to you?
18. How do the professional opportunities abroad compare with those in Türkiye?
19. Have your expectations been met since migrating? Please explain.

Section V: Migration Process and Challenges

20. What challenges did you face while migrating and adapting to a new country?
21. Did any institutions, companies, or personal networks help or hinder your transition?

Section VI: Reflections and Future Plans

22. Do you see yourself returning to Türkiye in the future? Why or why not?
23. What changes in Türkiye would make you consider coming back?
24. What advice would you give to other AI/IT professionals in Türkiye considering emigration?
25. Is there anything else you'd like to share about your experience?

References

Docquier, F., & Rapoport, H. (2012). Globalization, brain drain, and development. *Journal of Economic Literature, 50*(3), 681–730.

Fakih, A., & El Baba, M. (2023). *The decision to emigrate in six MENA countries: The role of post-revolutionary stress*. IZA Discussion Papers, No. 15933, Institute of Labor Economics (IZA), Bonn

Gürsoy, F., & Badur, B. (2021). An agent-based modeling approach to brain drain. *IEEE Transactions on Computational Social Systems, 9*(2), 356–365.

Metin, F. (2023). Brain drain from Türkiye: Register evidence of non-returning graduates. *Research in Educational Administration and Leadership, 8*(2), 373–419.

OECD. (2024). *International Migration Outlook 2024*. OECD Publishing. https://doi.org/10.1787/50b0353e-en

Öneri, İ. (2019). Türkiye'den beyin göçü (2007–2017). T.C. Pamukkale Üniversitesi Eğitim Bilimleri Enstitüsü, Eğitim Bilimleri Anabilim Dalı, Eğitim Yönetimi, Denetimi, Planlaması ve Ekonomisi Bilim Dalı.

Tansel, A., & Demet Güngör, N. (2003). "Brain drain" from Turkey: Survey evidence of student non-return. *Career Development International, 8*(2), 52–69.

TÜBITAK. (2025). 2236-A Uluslararası Deneyimli Araştırmacı Dolaşımı Destek Programı (CoCirculation3)—2025 Yılı Çağrısı. https://tubitak.gov.tr/tr/duyuru/2236-uluslararasi-deneyimli-arastirmaci-dolasimi-destek-programi-cocirculation3-2025-yili-cagrisi-yayinlandi

TÜIK. (2023). Eğitim Harcamaları Istatistikleri, 2023. Türkiye İstatistik Kurumu . Retrieved June 28, 2025, from https://data.tuik.gov.tr/Bulten/Index?p=Egitim-Harcamalari-Istatistikleri-2023-53557

TÜIK. (2024). *Göç İstatistikleri*. Türkiye İstatistik Kurumu Retrieved June 28, 2025, from https://data.tuik.gov.tr/Bulten/Index?p=Uluslararasi-Goc-Istatistikleri-2024-54083&dil=1

Wheatley, M. C. (2024). Navigating the digital divide: A global perspective. *Premier Journal of Computer Science, 1*, 100003.

YÖK. (2025). Yükseköğretim Bilgi Sistemi. Retrieved June 29, 2025, from https://istatistik.yok.gov.tr/

CHAPTER 6

Concluding Reflections: Assessing the Migration of Highly Skilled Professionals from Türkiye

Hasan Gürak

Introduction

This concluding chapter seeks to synthesize and critically assess the findings of the preceding analyses on the "migration of highly skilled professionals from Türkiye", framing the discussion within the structural dynamics that shape the position of less developed countries (LDCs) in the global economy. By integrating the empirical evidence and conceptual insights presented in earlier chapters, I aim to provide a comprehensive understanding of the phenomenon and its implications for Türkiye's long-term economic trajectory.

As outlined in my initial foundational contribution, the broader issue of "highly skilled professional migration" was initially examined through the lens of LDCs and characterized as a form of **"new-age imperialism,"** a structural process that systematically redistributes highly skilled professionals to the benefit of developed economies (DCs) while exacerbating

H. Gürak (✉)
Independent Researcher, Istanbul, Türkiye

H. Gürak (ed.), *The Economics of Migration of Highly Skilled Workers from Türkiye*,
https://doi.org/10.1007/978-3-032-10606-3_6

the developmental constraints of LDCs. The initial chapter emphasized that far from being a neutral flow of skills, this migration often operates as a mechanism that deepens global inequalities in incomes and economic performance.

Building on this theoretical foundation, the subsequent chapters offered progressively detailed investigations into the Turkish case. Chapter 2 analyzed the structural drivers and immediate causes of the "migration of highly skilled professionals from Türkiye," highlighting the interplay of domestic constraints and external opportunities. Chapter 3 turned to the medical sector, examining why highly educated physicians and nurses choose to emigrate and assessing the economic and social costs of their departure. Chapter 4 focused on engineers and technicians, professions central to technological upgrading and industrial development, and evaluated the negative repercussions of their loss. Chapter 5 investigated the increasingly critical outflow of AI and IT specialists, whose expertise has become indispensable to contemporary production and innovation systems, and whose absence poses mounting challenges for Türkiye's developmental prospects.

Having examined each of these dimensions individually, we are now positioned to evaluate the broader implications of these findings in an integrated manner. Several critical themes emerge. First, the migration of highly skilled professionals constitutes not merely an individual or sectoral loss but a structural transfer of productive capacity from Türkiye to advanced economies. Second, the cumulative effect of this transfer undermines Türkiye's ability to sustain endogenous innovation, upgrade its industrial base, and compete effectively in knowledge-intensive sectors. Finally, this dynamic raises pressing questions about the fairness and sustainability of a global economic system in which highly qualified professionals (for some, human capital), the most valuable economic assets of LDCs, continues to be drawn toward the already DCs.

Before turning to a forward-looking discussion, it is necessary to return to the central question that underpins this entire inquiry:

Which countries stand in greater need of "highly skilled professionals"?

Is it Türkiye itself?

Or the DCs, such as the USA, Germany, Sweden, and France, that, through migration, acquire Türkiye's most valuable economic assets, namely, its highly skilled professionals?

Assessing the Findings from the Perspective of the Turkish Economy

The initial chapter adopts a firm and principled stance against the migration of highly skilled professionals from LDCs to DCs, arguing that this process functions systematically to the advantage of DCs while operating to the detriment of LDCs.

The author identifies the primary drivers of this brain drain as fundamentally economic. The pursuit of higher living standards, access to improved working conditions, and the promise of better career opportunities constitute the most salient factors motivating this economically driven migration. Inadequate economic conditions and limited prospects in LDCs, especially when contrasted with the opportunities available in DCs, continue to push highly skilled individuals to seek employment and livelihoods abroad. Addressing this issue, the author argues that it requires coordinated global interventions; without such measures, the structural imbalances underlying highly skilled migration are unlikely to abate.

For LDCs, the loss of highly skilled professionals represents the erosion of their most critical developmental resource. These individuals embody the knowledge, expertise, and creative capacity indispensable for sustained economic growth and structural transformation. Their continued outflow undermines national efforts to achieve self-sustaining development, perpetuating dependence on external sources of technology and innovation.

The author conceptualizes this process as a form of "***New-Age Imperialism.***" Historically, developed countries exerted control over raw materials and labor in their colonies to secure economic advantage. In contemporary times, they extend this control to what has become the most valuable resource of all: highly skilled human capital. Through favorable institutional and economic arrangements, DCs effectively extract and appropriate the intellectual assets of LDCs, further entrenching global hierarchies of knowledge and production.

From author's perspective, this exploitative structure, embodied in the "migration of highly skilled professionals," must not only be halted but ultimately reversed. He maintains that LDCs require these highly skilled professionals far more urgently than DCs if they are to accelerate economic development and close the persistent gap in income and economic capacity. Without a critical mass of qualified and creative professionals, sustainable development and meaningful reductions in global inequality remain unattainable.

In summary, Gürak regards the outflow of highly skilled professionals as a deeply damaging mechanism of exploitation. Far from being a neutral or mutually beneficial process, it constitutes a structural barrier that constrains the developmental trajectories of LDCs while reinforcing the systemic advantages of DCs. For Türkiye, as for other LDCs, the challenge lies in devising effective global strategies to retain and mobilize its most valuable economic assets, its highly skilled professionals, toward the pursuit of national development goals.

Chapter 2 delves into the underlying factors motivating the migration of highly skilled professionals from Türkiye to DCs, a phenomenon of growing concern for the country's economic and social development. The chapter's authors, F. Topal and Z. Hopyar, present a nuanced framework that identifies both structural and individual determinants of this migration process, emphasizing the interplay of "push" and "pull" dynamics.

According to the authors, the decision to migrate rarely stems from a single cause; rather, it emerges at the intersection of economic, political, social, and cultural factors. On the "push" side, structural issues within Türkiye, such as limited professional opportunities, insufficient compensation, and systemic inefficiencies, create significant disincentives for highly skilled individuals to migrate. These conditions are compounded by broader political and sociocultural concerns, including restricted personal freedoms and perceived limitations on career advancement, all of which collectively erode the sense of professional fulfillment and long-term security.

Conversely, the "pull" factors associated with DCs exert a powerful attraction. Higher living standards, access to advanced professional development opportunities, and substantially more competitive salaries serve as primary economic incentives for migration. Beyond pure financial considerations, meritocratic institutional environments, transparent and rules-based systems, and the safeguarding of political and personal freedoms in destination countries further enhance their appeal.

Topal and Hopyar argue that any strategy aimed at curbing the outflow of highly skilled professionals must engage with this complex constellation of factors. Economic reforms alone, while necessary, are unlikely to suffice; durable solutions must address the structural, political, and cultural conditions that shape the aspirations and career trajectories of highly skilled individuals. Only by confronting these root causes comprehensively can Türkiye hope to retain the highly skilled professionals essential for its long-term economic growth and economic competitiveness.

Chapter 3 examines the emigration of highly skilled healthcare professionals, such as doctors and nurses, from Türkiye. According to the findings of the chapter's authors, S. Tauscher and Y. Eskicioğlu, the brain drain of healthcare professionals has reached alarming proportions over the past decade. Data from the Turkish Medical Association (TTB) reveal a striking increase in the number of physicians obtaining "good standing" certificates required to work abroad: from only 90 in 2013 to 3025 in the first 11 months of 2023, with the total number for the last decade reaching 5035. This sharp rise indicates a critical turning point, particularly in the period following 2016–2017.

Türkiye consistently ranks near the bottom among OECD countries in terms of the number of doctors and nurses per 1000 inhabitants. According to 2021 OECD data, Türkiye has only 2.2 physicians per 1000 people, compared to the OECD average of 3.7. The disparity is even greater for nurses: fewer than 3 nurses per 1000 people in Türkiye versus an OECD average of 9.2. These figures starkly highlight the existing human resource gap in the Turkish healthcare system.

The costs of brain drain for Türkiye are considerable. The state invests substantial resources in the education of healthcare professionals, for example, the inflation-adjusted six-year training cost of a single medical student for the 2009–2010 academic year is estimated at approximately USD 180,000. In addition, there are "hidden" expenditures, including infrastructure and staffing costs of university hospitals, which further compound the economic burden of this migration.

The loss of qualified healthcare personnel weakens the healthcare infrastructure, leading to service disruptions, particularly in rural areas, and deteriorating maternal and child health outcomes.

Tauscher and Eskicioğlu stress that the brain drain among Türkiye's healthcare professionals is a multifaceted and complex phenomenon, driven by the interplay of push factors within Türkiye and pull factors in developed countries. They conclude that this dynamic imposes significant socio-economic costs on Türkiye, exacerbating existing challenges in both healthcare delivery and human capital retention.

In Chap. 4, authors H. Gökırmak and F. Sekmen investigate the emigration of engineers and technicians from Türkiye and assess its implications for the national economy. After a detailed examination of the driving forces behind this migration, they arrive at several important conclusions.

Engineers and technicians hold a position of vital importance for the Turkish economy. They not only ensure the effective utilization of existing technologies but also spearhead the development of new ones, thereby fueling development. Their contributions enhance productivity, enabling Turkish industries to become more competitive in global markets. By creating highly skilled employment opportunities, they attract investment to the country and help boost exports.

The migration of engineers and technicians, however, poses serious negative consequences for Türkiye's economy. Foremost among these is the loss of highly trained professionals (in their terms human capital), which hampers productivity and undermines overall economic performance. It slows GDP growth and disproportionately affects sectors that rely heavily on technological advancement, engineering, and advanced manufacturing. Furthermore, it exacerbates labor shortages in critical sectors, raising operational costs for businesses. In the long term, this outflow erodes the country's innovation capacity, leads to slower economic growth, and diminishes Türkiye's global competitiveness.

Gökırmak and Sekmen conclude that the migration of engineers and technicians presents a major challenge for Türkiye, one that threatens its technological progress, economic resilience, and long-term development prospects.

In Chap. 5, the authors, Gökırmak and Sekmen, focus on the emigration of artificial intelligence (AI) and information technology (IT) specialists from Türkiye, a trend of growing strategic importance given the increasing role of these professions in production and economic development. They begin by examining the structural and individual drivers behind this migration and then assess its broader implications for Türkiye's economy.

AI and IT professionals are critical to foster digital transformation, advancing technological capabilities, and enhancing the innovation capacity of the economy. They play a pivotal role in the development of high value-added sectors, helping domestic industries remain competitive in an increasingly knowledge-driven global marketplace. Their expertise supports productivity growth, attracts foreign investment, and facilitates the creation of new, technology-intensive employment opportunities.

However, the emigration of these highly skilled professionals imposes substantial costs on Türkiye. The loss of digital talent slows the adoption of advanced technologies and weakens the country's innovation ecosystem. It creates severe skill shortages in critical sectors, driving up operational costs for businesses and deterring technology-intensive investments. Over time, this outflow threatens to widen the technological gap between

Türkiye and DCs undermining long-term economic growth and competitiveness.

The authors emphasize that the migration of AI and IT professionals represents not only a loss of highly skilled professionals (human capital) but also a strategic challenge for Türkiye's development. Addressing this issue requires comprehensive policies aimed at improving the domestic environment for innovation, offering competitive opportunities for digital specialists, and creating conditions conducive to retaining and attracting top-tier technological talent.

Conclusions

This chapter presents a holistic evaluation of the findings discussed in the previous chapters, synthesizing insights on the migration of highly skilled professionals from Türkiye and its implications for the country's economic future. The emigration of highly skilled professionals from Türkiye results in multifaceted challenges. It exacerbates labor shortages in high-technology and specialized sectors, hindering the operational capacity of businesses and escalating costs, especially within critical industries like manufacturing and information technology. This highly skilled labor deficit diminishes Türkiye's attractiveness to investors and impairs its competitiveness in the global marketplace. The consequent decline in overall productivity slows GDP growth and restricts the advancement of high value-added industries. In short, from the perspective of LDCs, the loss of critical professionals constitutes a significant obstacle to sustainable economic growth and development.

Conversely, developed countries benefit substantially from this inflow of highly skilled professionals, securing vital talent necessary for technological innovation and maintaining their competitive edge. This dynamic reflects a form of contemporary "**new-age imperialism**," whereby DCs continue to appropriate the most valuable human resources from LDCs under conditions favorable to themselves.

Based on the examples of Türkiye, it is worth repeating and emphasizing the following regarding the "migration of highly skilled professionals":

> ***LDCs** are increasingly losing their most valuable assets, **SMLs**, to **DCs** due to migration of highly skilled professionals, as a result of self-centered and unethical policies in **DCs**, given the economic conditions in **LDCs**. If the migration*

> *trend continues as it is today,* ***LDCs*** *will continue to suffer severe economic losses in terms of* ***SML****, while* ***DCs*** *will be the winners at the lowest possible cost. And the convergence of global incomes will remain a utopian wish.* (Chap. 1, in this book)

The current migration trends represent a major challenge that calls for comprehensive policy interventions aimed at retention and the return of highly skilled professionals to foster national development and reduce global inequalities.

DCs are well aware of the economic value of highly skilled labor and therefore make every effort to transfer them to their countries to serve their people.

But What About the Needs of Developing Countries?

DCs must set aside their selfish and imperialist/colonialist mentality and actively contribute, together with LDCs, to the formation of a new global order that is more equitable and sustainable. To this end, a new framework regarding the migration of highly skilled professionals should be established, accompanied by effective policy measures and interventions.

What Happens If This Colonialist Mindset Persists?
In the long run, migration from LDCs to DCs will become unstoppable, with all types of "economic refugees" attempting to move to DCs. The consequences will extend beyond demographic shifts in DCs, triggering a wide range of social, psychological, and global economic problems. The scale, diversity, and severity of these issues will intensify, leading to significant social challenges in the receiving countries.

The critical question guiding this analysis was: Who needs the highly skilled professional more?

1. Developing countries? or
2. Developed countries

Index[1]

[1] Note: Page numbers followed by 'n' refer to notes.

H. Gürak (ed.), *The Economics of Migration of Highly Skilled Workers from Türkiye*,
https://doi.org/10.1007/978-3-032-10606-3

FSC
www.fsc.org
MIX
Papier | Fördert
gute Waldnutzung
FSC® C083411

Kolibri 360 GmbH
Ferdinand-Jühlke-Straße 7
99095 Erfurt, Deutschland
produktsicherheit@kolibri360.de